SPIRIT AND REALITY

NICOLAS BERDYAEV

Spirit and Reality

⊕

Foreword *Boris Jakim*
Translator *George Reavey*

San Rafael CA

First Edition, Geoffrey Bles, Ltd., London, 1939
Second, enlarged edition, Semantron Press, 2009
Semantron is an imprint of Sophia Perennis LLC
Foreword and Biography © Boris Jakim 2009

For information, address:
Semantron Press, P.O. Box 151011
San Rafael, CA 94915
semantronpress.com

Library of Congress Cataloging-in-Publication Data

Berdiaev, Nikolai, 1874–1948.
[Dukh i realnost. English]
Spirit and reality / Nicolas Berdyaev.—2nd enl. ed.

p. cm.
Originally published: London: Geoffrey Bles, 1939.
Includes index.
ISBN 978 1 59731 254 7 (pbk: alk. paper)
1. Spirituality. 2. Civilization—Philosophy. 3. Metaphysics. I. Title.
BV5409.R8B43 2009
233'.5—dc22   2009022491

Cover photograph by Dorlys Paris

CONTENTS

Foreword 3

CHAPTER I. The Reality of the Spirit 7

CHAPTER II. The Attributes of Spirit 33

CHAPTER III. The Objectification of Spirit. Symbolization
and Realization 49

CHAPTER IV. The Aim of Asceticism 69

CHAPTER V. Evil and Suffering as Problems of Spirit 93

CHAPTER VI. Mysticism: Its Contradictions and
Achievements 117

CHAPTER VII. The New Spirituality. The Realization
of Spirit 147

Index 179

A Brief Overview of Nikolai Berdyaev's Life and Works 183

Bibliography of Nikolai Berdyaev's Books in English
Translation (in alphabetical order) 190

FOREWORD

In *Spirit and Reality*, Nikolai[1] Berdyaev explores the nature of spirit, describes how modernity has obscured the true meaning of spirit by distorting objectifications and symbolizations, and tells how human creative activity, in concert with divine activity, can overcome these distortions and lead us into the kingdom of authentic spiritual life. In other words, he tells us that spirit is real, whereas the objectified world around us is not real.

For Berdyaev, spirit is a dynamic force transcending frontiers and limitations. Spirit in man should not be confused with soul or mind; it is that which is divine in man and comes from and participates in the divine Spirit (that which Christians call the Holy Spirit). The spiritual dimension in man is the dimension of freedom. It is also the dimension of creative activity: "Every creative act is a spiritual act" (p. 56, present volume). However, in the objectified[2] world the spirit and its creative activity have only a symbolical structure; that is, in the objectified world we have the symbolization of spirit, whereas we must seek the realization of spirit: "The whole of man's moral and ethical life is a symbolical structure rather than a real transfiguration of

---

1. "Nikolai" is the more correct form of Berdyaev's first name. The original translations of Berdyaev's works into English used "Nicolas"; in order to avoid confusion this spelling is retained on the cover and title page.

2. What is "objectification"? According to Berdyaev, we are cast into a world of objects, into an objective world, which has a metaphysical meaning for us. This objectification is the fall of the world: the loss of the world's freedom, the alienation of its parts. The world of appearances (of objects) acquires a grandiose empirical reality which exercises compulsion upon us. These objectified constructions begin to live an independent life and give rise to pseudo-realities. Even though it is our own construction, we cannot escape this objectified world; we too can become objectified—parts of this objectified world, slaves to it. In Berdyaev's own words: "Objectification is the ejection of man into the external; it is his exteriorization; it is his subjugation to the conditions of space, time, causality, and rationalization" (p. 60, *The Beginning and the End*).

human beings" (p. 62, present volume). We know and experience not what is real, but symbols for what is real.

Symbolization affects even what we hold sacred: "Sanctification is invariably symbolization. In this world sanctity is not a sacred reality, but the symbol of the sacred reality. The historical objectification of spirit gives rise to the sanctification of certain elements of natural and human life: to the sanctification of the state, the nation, the family, property, society, culture, etc. Such symbolical sanctification also characterizes the churches and ecclesial rituals of the world: "Sanctity is symbolized in anointed hierarchs, in material objects sprinkled with holy water" (p. 63, present volume). But what is one to do? How does one escape the objectification and symbolization of the world and even of the spirit?

According to Berdyaev, what is needed is a new spirituality. Our present world is experiencing a weakening and diminishing spirituality as a result of the increasing objectification of human existence: human beings have stopped being spiritual subjects; they have become objects, indistinguishable from the other objects of the world. The aim of the new spirituality would be to replenish the diminishing spirituality, to halt and reverse the progressive objectification of the world. The new spirituality would signify freedom from objectification and from the subjection of spirit to the influence of a wicked and fallen society. It would also imply a transition from spiritual symbolism to spiritual realization. How is the new spirituality to be realized? Berdyaev does not tell us this in detail, but he certainly tells us that it can be achieved only in freedom and through the efforts of our creative inner self-transfiguration and of the creative transfiguration of the objectified world.

According to Berdyaev, Christianity too has been afflicted by objectification and symbolization, and needs to undergo further spiritualization. It needs to attain a purer form of spirituality which will liberate man from the pathological idea that God is moved by human suffering, e.g., in the torments of ascetics and martyrs. God needs not the suffering, fear, and servitude of human beings, but their ascension, their ecstatic transcendence of their limitations. The new spirituality will be an experience of creative energy and inspiration, where the symbolism associated with human slavery and limitation will be discarded. The aim of the spiritual life is to overcome egocentricity, to realize the personality through self-transcendence. And in overcoming egocentricity, spirituality directs man's energies toward his fellow beings, toward society and the world in general. For Berdyaev, this is the true teaching of the Gospel. This is a new Gospel, concerned not only with the past, with Christ and with the evil world that crucified Him, but also with the future, with Christ's Second Coming, with the Kingdom of God. However, the Second Coming, the Kingdom of God is not only a divine work, but is also being prepared by human activity and creativeness; the end of the world is man's responsibility as well as God's. God's action in the world is revealed through the human spirit.

In concluding, Berdyaev tells us that the purified, liberated spirituality will be a subjectification, a passage into the sphere of pure existence. The objectified world can be destroyed by the joint creative effort of man and God. This will require a change in human consciousness, inasmuch as the phantom world of objects is the creation of a falsely oriented consciousness. This great change will lead us into the kingdom of the spirit; we will live in a form of ascending and descending spiritual realism, active rather than passive in spirit. God will descend down to us, and we will ascend to him on the wings of our creative spirit.

BORIS JAKIM
2008

CHAPTER I

THE REALITY OF SPIRIT
SPIRIT AND BEING

I

While refusing to doubt the reality of immediately perceptible phenomena the world tends, on the whole, to deny the reality of spirit. But spirit is not an immediately perceptible phenomenon, an object among other objects. It is true that all men, even the most materially minded, acknowledge a minimum of spiritual reality. They could hardly do otherwise, since even those are endowed with the spirit who repudiate it. But in such cases spirit is treated as an epiphenomenon, although no adequate explanation has ever been offered of this process. The materialistic denial of spirit is ultimately an inexact description of the data of experienced realities, as inexact, say, as a Daltonist description of world phenomena. The materialist glosses over the real difficulties by attributing to matter all the qualities inherent in spirit—namely, reason, freedom, energy. More subtle philosophies regard spirit as an epiphenomenon of life endowed with an inexhaustible creative energy. That is a vitalistic interpretation of spirit. Spiritualistic philosophies, on the other hand, have made it their business to defend the reality of spirit. Spiritualism usually interprets spirit as a substance, a reality of a peculiar kind in the natural world. Philosophical thought has often naturalized spirit, situating it as the highest stage in the hierarchy of the objective world. In this context spirit is an object of a higher order, but still an object. Thus spirit was regarded as an objective reality. But is spiritual reality demonstrable like objective reality? Therein lies the difficulty of the problem confronting us. Philosophy has a tendency to objectify and to hypostasize

7

thought, to identify reality with objectivity. A demonstration of spiritual reality becomes a demonstration of its objectivity. Those who deny the reality of spirit commonly maintain that spirit is merely a subjective state of the individual soul. They identify the manifestations of spirit with psychic or subjective manifestations. Hence those who affirm the reality of spirit are anxious to demonstrate the objective nature of spiritual manifestations. Spiritualistic ontology claims that authentic or essential being is spirit; and that spirit is being, objective being.

But what is being? That is the fundamental problem of philosophy. We are prone to think of being as something indubitable and axiomatic. But the critique of knowledge poses a further problem, that of the influence exercised by mental processes on our conception of being, that of the extent to which the agency of the subject helps to elaborate a conception of so-called 'primal' being. That was the problem which Kant set out to solve; and his great achievements in this direction, since ignored or deformed by Neo-Kantianism, are now worthy of being rehabilitated. Kant was not an idealist in the current sense of the word; his researches were directed to the discovery of reality. In his philosophy are laid the foundations of the only true metaphysics: a dualism of the spheres of freedom and nature; voluntarism, indeterminism, personalism; the doctrine of antinomies; the avowal of another manifest, deeper reality hidden from the world. The German metaphysicians of the early nineteenth century, Fichte, Schelling and Hegel, were too eager to oppose monistic systems of thought to Kantian dualism. But Kantian dualism contains a greater element of eternal truth than monism, which is a type of self-objectifying and self-hypostasizing thought. Metaphysics is rather apt to hypostasize concepts, and then to interpret them as if they were being. The aim of ontology is to discover objective being. But it actually discovers an objectified concept; it perceives an objective being which is the product of its own elaborated concepts. Thus ontology appears to be able to apprehend only a conceptional and already rationalized being. In the category of being knowledge may be a form of naturalist metaphysics. By Naturalism I mean any metaphysical system which conceives being objectively, as 'nature', even when it may be spiritual nature. In the Kantian system there are, however, the latent possibilities of an existential philosophy emancipated from any kind of naturalistic metaphysics. Kant himself did not exploit these possibilities to the full. Early nineteenth century German Idealism was too much penetrated by Kantian criticism to develop the theses of the dogmatic pre-Kantian naturalist metaphysics; instead it postulated the subject as the means of exploring the mystery of being. But German metaphysics was on the whole deformed by its monistic and evolutionary bias for identifying spirit and nature, and for affirming the existence of an objective spirit. In Hegel's very remarkable dialectic, being is a most abstract and empty concept, synonymous with non-being. This notion led him to discover *becoming*, the development of the world-spirit, whereas other and quite different conclusions might have been drawn therefrom. In its preoccupation with the universal impersonal spirit German Idealist metaphysics failed to consider the problem of man and that of his personality. It helped the universal concept —a general idea, but not in the sense understood by Greek philosophy—to triumph over the individual, the unique, and the authentically existential. Thus the philosophy of spirit became that of objective being. The rational concept of being continued to hold sway. In a certain sense Schopenhauer was better orientated despite the contradictory nature of his philosophy. The fundamental fact must be faced, that the existential apprehension of being does not coincide with the objective-naturalistic one; they are, in fact, antithetical. Fichte's theory of the primal Ego approximates to this conception, but he persisted, on the other hand, in upholding the universalist and anti-personalist position. The mystery of reality is not solved by concentrating on the object, but by reflecting on the action of the subject.

We are now confronted with the following problem: Is a rationally elaborated category of being applicable to the spirit, to God? Apophatic mystical theology would deny that the category of being is applicable to God, for it conceives God as super-being or even non-being. This conception should also be applied, though in a different way, to the philosophy of spirit. Spirit is neither an objective reality nor a rational category of being. Spirit has never existed, nor can it exist anywhere, in the form of a real object. The philosophy of spirit should not be a philosophy of being or an ontology, but a philosophy of existence. Spirit is not only a reality of a different kind from that of the natural spirit or that of objects, but it is an altogether different reality. To make use of Kantian terminology—in which, incidentally, the word '*spirit*' does not occur—we may affirm that the reality of spirit is that of freedom rather than that of nature. Spirit is never an object; nor is spiritual reality an objective one. In the so-called objective world there is no such nature, thing, or objective reality as spirit. Hence it is easy to deny the reality of spirit. God is spirit because He is not object, because He is subject. Many would agree with this. But the same is true of spirit. Spirit is revealed in the subject, whereas in the object we can only discern an objectified spirit. Spirit inheres only in the subject, who alone is existential. The object is the projection of the subject, the result of objectifying processes. The subject is divinely created, and he is therefore endowed with primary existence. The subject is a mental concept only when he is opposed to the object conceived correlatively, but not as part of his inner existence. But pure spirituality exists independently of the intellectual opposition of subject and object. Therefore spirit is not in the least subjective, although it exists only in the subject. In contrast to objectivity, it is not subjective in the psychological sense of the word. The reality of spirit is not an objective one, but a reality of another kind, an immeasurably greater one, a more primal one. We must be careful not to interpret this in the sense of abstract spiritualism which opposes spirit to the realities of the body and the soul, with the result that spirit suppresses or denies the body and the soul, and becomes situated in the same category of natural realities as the body and the soul. But spirit leads a higher qualitative existence than the body or the soul. The threefold conception of man as a spiritual, psychic and corporeal being, has a permanent validity. This does not mean, however, that man's spiritual nature is on the same level as his psychic and corporeal natures, but it does imply that his soul and body can participate in a new and higher order of spiritual existence, that man is able to pass from the natural order to that of freedom, from the region of discord and hostility to that of love, union and meaning. Man is a spiritual being, filled with spiritual energy, but he has no objective spiritual nature or substance comparable to his psychic or corporeal substance. The human body, too, can exist in spirit, it can be spiritualized. The spiritual principle is not an objective one. An object exists for the subject, it is objectively manifest only for the subject. But spiritual reality has another genesis—a non-objective reality imparted by God. Who is subject. My inner spiritual reality is not an object. I cannot be an object in relation to myself. The subject is not a substance, a naturalistic category, but an act. The spiritual sphere excludes the opposition of thought and being, the objectification and hypostasis of concepts. The spirit reflects the truth of the soul, its eternal validity. In this sense, spirit is axiological and evaluative. Spirituality is the highest quality, a value, man's highest achievement. Spirit is not another actuality, but it informs actuality with purpose. Spirit is, as it were, a Divine breath, penetrating human existence and endowing it with the highest dignity, with the highest quality of existence, with an inner independence and unity. An objective interpretation of spiritual reality raises the question: Do my spiritual states and experiences correspond to any authentic reality or are they merely subjective states? But this is a fundamentally false presentation of the problem, one based on the supposition that the subject should reflect some sort of object. Actually, spiritual states do not correspond to anything, they simply *are*; they are the prime reality, they are more existential than anything reflected in the objective world.

The distinction between spiritual reality and reality in general depends on the solution of the problem of the relation between thought and being. Realism and Idealism are the two classic solutions. Scholasticism and Thomism are a classical form of Realism. In the nineteenth and twentieth centuries Realism becomes warped and corrupted. Thomist Realism consciously endeavoured to be a naïve Realism; it critically repudiates the critique of knowledge, the attempt to discover to what extent the agency of the subject influences our interpretation and knowledge of the world. We tend to accept as reality what is, in fact, an elaboration on the part of the subject, an objectified concept. A consistent, conscious, critical Realism should postulate the absolute passivity of the subject. Accordingly knowledge appears to be wholly determined by the object, and thought merely serves to reflect the object. In this light it is difficult to grasp how a material object can become a subject, the intellectual phenomenon of knowing. It is a grave error to postulate only Realism and Idealism as the two active principles of the theory of knowledge. The first regards knowledge as being wholly determined by the object as the authentic reality; the second apprehends the world as being merely a construction of the subject. Actually, Realism and Idealism are not the only alternatives, for there is a third position which I personally consider to be the only valid one. When defending the philosophy of the object, the realist critics of Idealism are inclined to forget that the activity of the subject is not altogether identical with thought, that the subject himself participates in being, that he is existential, that he can achieve an authentic knowledge of reality. We are therefore not really confronted with the dilemma of either postulating the authentic reality of an object absorbed by the knowing subject or denying external reality altogether by breaking it up into a series of sensations and concepts formed by the subject. The subject himself is being—if we have to use this term—and the only authentic being is that of the subject. The subject is more than merely thought; he is voluntarist and existential. The part played by the will in knowledge is tremendous. It is entirely wrong to say that the world is created by the subject, for the world is created by God; but God creates living, creative subjects rather than objects or things. The subject does not create the world, but he is called upon to create in the world. From the authentic existential standpoint reality is not a creation of knowledge, but knowledge is a creative art. Objective reality depends on the knowing subject, on his existential character. Apprehensible reality varies in accordance with a man's existential quality or his relationship to other men—in other words, apprehension is a social fact. It is essential to determine what the creative subject contributes to knowledge. In essence both subjective and absolute Idealism agree in denying man's creative rôle in knowledge. Their creative subject is not man, but rather the transcendental consciousness, the general consciousness, the supra-personal subject, the absolute spirit. In a world thus created there is no longer room for human creativeness. It is an error to associate Realism invariably with the object, with objective things. There is also a Realism of the subject, derived from the existential subject. Knowledge is not simply the relation of thought to being, since that would involve the primacy of thought, which is not being, over being itself. Knowledge is an event within being, an event revealing the mystery of being. But this is a non-objectified, non-exteriorized being. Spirit is the reality revealed in and through the existential subject, a reality emanating from within rather than from without, from the objective world. The object is formulated by the subject in the process of objectifying concepts; for the subject finds himself in a state of corruption, in a state of division and discord with other subjects, with the Divine world, with the cosmos. But this is very

B

different from the activity of the subject as interpreted by Idealism. Scholastic and rationalistic Realism is an optimistic theory of knowledge which does not take sufficiently into account the fallen and disintegrated state of the world and man. Spirit triumphs over this state of affairs. In this connection we should also consider another aspect of Realism—the Platonic and Scholastic problem of the reality of the universals. The two problems are interrelated. Conceptional Realism is blind to the active contribution of thought, of the subject—that is, it fails to perceive the process of objectification. But, as we shall see, the exclusive choice between Realism and Nominalism is quite as erroneous as the exclusive choice between Realism and Idealism.

The realism of objects is more closely related to the realism of concepts than is commonly stated in the history of philosophy. The realism of spirit is not that of an object. But is the realism of spirit that of the universals or that of the general? In the history of the concept, '*spirit*', an important part was played by the interpretation of spirituality as the sum of the universal, general principles of human life as distinct from the particular and the individual. The world has ideal foundations of a universal character, and these are also its spiritual foundations (such, for example, as the ideal-realism of N. Lossky and Franck; such also is Sophiology). This doctrine can be traced back to Plato. It lends itself to a hypostasis of abstract concepts, to an objectification of concepts. The *objectivity*, as distinct from the *subjectivity*, of everything particular and individual serves mostly as the ideal spiritual foundation of the world. In this way a spiritual conception diametrically opposed to the existential one is evolved. This is the objective, universal spirit, the source of an all-binding knowledge of the universals. Actually, it would be correct to define spirit as something opposed to the general, the objectified and the impersonal. The reality of the universals confirmed the reality of the general and the abstract, the inherence in objects of what is affirmed in concepts claiming universal validity. The reality of the universals is an objectified one; or, in other words, there are no primal realities inherent in the universals. The primal realities are always existential. The universals have no real existence. But it is also an error to identify the universal and the general. The general is an abstraction, whereas the universal is concrete in the authentic sense of the word and implies a fullness and wealth of content lacking in bare abstraction. The debates of the realists and the nominalists failed to make this fact sufficiently clear. It would be a mistake to oppose the realism of the Universals to Nominalism, which is another pole of abstraction. Nominalism is essentially incapable of apprehending the realities of the particular, the personal and the concrete, for it is involved in a process of infinite analysis which prevents it from grasping anything real or whole. Both Realism and Nominalism are equally abstract, and fail to detect any reality in the universal or the particular. Universalist Realism is obliged to postulate the generic nature of everything particular. Hence everything particular is secondary and derivative. Platonism is likewise a philosophy of generic being, and, as a result, it is unable to pose the problem of the personality. Nominalism, since it is involved in a process of infinite analysis, is equally powerless to postulate the independence, the integrity and the primacy of individual being, to pose the problem of the personality.

Logical Universalism usually recruits its defenders from among those who are anxious to preserve knowledge from the ravages of extreme Nominalism and Empiricism. But they are likewise the victims of illusion. For actuality is individual, irrational and, above all, primal; integral actuality is precisely that which has authentic existence. This actuality appears to be impenetrable to logical Universalism which is exclusively preoccupied with the general. The concept is a generalization, an abstraction. General and abstract concepts are the result of objectifying processes in knowledge. But man also endeavours to apprehend the concrete-particular and the concrete-universal, as distinct from the abstract-universal. Logical Universalism with its reliance on abstract concepts fails to achieve this end. In this consists the tragedy of knowledge upon which Kant more than anyone else insisted. The problem of irrational knowledge owes a great deal to the work of German philosophy. Is a rational apprehension of the irrational possible? There is, indeed, a knowledge independent of the conceptional apprehension of objects on the premise of universal principles, a knowledge penetrating existence and concrete actuality, a knowledge which is at once a participation in being and an illumination of life. And this is the only way of apprehending spirit, the ever-concrete spirit. Spirit is not involved in the opposition between the general and the generic on the one hand and the particular and the individual on the other, which was the bone of contention in the disputations of the Nominalists and the Realists. The knowledge of spirit is different in kind from that of objective nature. The opposition of the subjective and the objective, of the general and the particular, of the generic and the individual, does not affect the spirit or spirituality. It is a mistake to attribute to spirit symptoms discerned in objective nature, for this only helps to naturalize spirit. Spirit is not the ideal, universal premise of the world. It is concrete, personal and *subjective*; it reveals itself in personal existence, just as the concrete-universal spirit reveals itself in personal existence. The concrete-universal content can be detected in the personal existence, in its highest qualities and plenitude, rather than in any ideal abstract sphere or in any generic existence of ideas. Spirit should be interpreted above all in a personalistic way. From the existential standpoint, the sphere of the personality is quite different from that of the opposition between the general and the particular, the universal and individual. The personality is individually unique, separate, distinct, unlike anything else, possessed of a universal content, capable of embracing the world with its love and understanding. Spirit comes to life only in this sphere, unrelated as yet to any ideal universal principles. Far from being rooted in the universals or any ideal world, the personal spirit is a Divine image. But although the spirit and spirituality are extra-generic, they can influence generic existence. To postulate a universal and generic existence for the spirit is equivalent to denying freedom and admitting a certain measure of determinism. But spirit is freedom. It cannot be determined by any Platonic world of ideas. Men have likened the spirit to a breath, to a Divine inspiration, but this is hardly consistent with logical Universalism. Man discovers his freedom above all in spirit; therein he is free not only from natural and social determination, but also from that of logical Universalism. Hegel realized the meaning of freedom, *being-in-oneself*, that spirit is an eternal return to oneself. Spirit should never be identified with monism, but that has frequently been the case in the history of thought, Hegel himself not excepted. The existence of spirit even postulates dualism. But this dualism is not that of God and man, of the Creator and the creature, but rather one of the subjective and the objective, of freedom and determination, of spirit and nature, of the personal and the general.

Spirit cannot be determined by the universals, but it does imply man's endeavour to emerge from his confinement and to grasp the concrete-universal. Spirit is a personal revelation, but it endows the personality with a supra-personal content. It is also a subjective revelation, but it preserves man from *subjectivity* in the worst sense of the word, from the inability to distinguish between realities and to participate in them. The reality of spirit is also an awareness of realities. Spirit is visionary and beholds realities, spiritual and objective, natural and psychological, historical and social. The fundamental attributes of the spiritual kingdom are the absence of generic, mass and collective elements, the fact that its content is both individual-personal and concrete-universal. These are also the signs of freedom and love. Of all realities spirit is the most real, since the subjective-personal is more real than the objective. When the claim is made that the universal laws of reason are the only justification of existence, then we are confronted with the conceptional as opposed to the existential. The reality of spirit cannot be apprehended in this manner. Spirit and spiritual reality are not governed by the universal laws of reason; they do not reflect the ideal universal or the objective world. Their world is the image of a concrete inner humanity, of an experience of human destiny, of human love and death, of human tragedy. A spiritualistic interpretation of spirit should postulate spirit as a reality of an absolutely different kind from that of objective thought and nature. Abstract spiritualism and idealism tend to divorce spirit from the fullness of life by transposing it into an *ideal* sphere which excludes the knowledge of an active and concrete spirit. Nor can spirit be adequately interpreted from the vitalist standpoint. It can, indeed, be affirmed that spirit is life, but only as long as this is not understood in the biological sense of the word. The spirit is primarily existential. There are various kinds of realities: physical, organic, psychological, social; and there are also realities like truth, goodness, beauty, value, creativeness, imagination. Truth is a reality, unlike natural or objective reality; it is a spiritual reality, a spiritual element in human existence. As opposed to a *ratio* or abstract thought, the integral human mind is spirit; it is spiritual, rooted in existence. There is an inherent spiritual *transcending* principle in man. Spirit is subject because subject is opposed to object. Fichte had grasped this fact. Spirit affirms its reality through man, who is a manifestation of spirit. Consciousness and self-consciousness are related to spirit. Consciousness is not merely a psychological concept, it contains a constructive spiritual element. Hence the possibility of a passage from consciousness to super-consciousness. Spirit is the agency of super-consciousness in consciousness. Spirit exercises a primacy over being.

II

The history of the term, spirit (*pneuma* and *nous*), may throw some light on its existence. It is a complex history. A spiritualizing tendency asserted itself only gradually in the conception of spirit. In the Holy Scripture spirit is a fundamental term. But originally spirit (*pneuma* in Greek, *ruah* in ancient Hebrew) had a physical connotation, meaning wind or breath. *Pneuma* was ethereal. *Ruah* also signifies something light, insubstantial, elusive. It is also a Divine breath, a Divine gift of life. Life depends on God, without Whom man has no life of his own. The human soul descends into the grave while *ruah* returns to God. The characteristic Platonic or Cartesian opposition of spirit and matter was alien to ancient Hebrew thought. For it the living creature was the body, holding within itself the spirit of life. That spirit emanated from and returned to God. In the Bible, as in Greek thought, the spirit was not inherent in man, but was a gift from on high. Thus *ruah* was dynamic. But we must distinguish between prophetic inspiration and the life-giving spirit. The Spirit of Javeh, the Divine Spirit, is the Divine power. Persian and Hellenic influences were chiefly responsible for the materialization and the hypostasis of spirit. And this led to the hypostasis of wisdom. In the Persian consciousness everything was motivated by the Spirit from on high. Spirit was breath and air, and it was also the breathing of living creatures, of men and gods. The Greeks had two words to denote spirit: *pneuma* and *nous*. *Pneuma*, like *ruah*, originally meant breath and breathing. *Pneuma* was also associated with fire. The Persians especially regarded *pneuma* as an element akin not only to sun and fire, but also to air and water. The ancients tended to represent spirit as a sort of fluid matter, and the conception of spirit as immaterial substance was of later growth. In the Gospel *pneuma* denoted both spirit and the Holy Spirit; but as interpreted by Aristotle and the Stoics it had material and physical attributes; these it acquired again in Plotinus, who employed the word *nous* to denote spirit. While *pneuma* was a current term in the poetical and popular idioms, *nous* acquired chiefly a philosophical currency. Anaxagoras's reasoning spirit, the fundamental principle of being, is *nous*. Philon's *pneuma* acquired a greater spiritual significance. He was, indeed, one of the first who attempted to define spirit. According to him, spirit is wise, Divine, indivisible, omnisensitive. It is a cosmic element— this is the consequence of likening it to air; it is also knowledge, wisdom, idea—this is an inheritance of Greek philosophy. Philon's spirit becomes an independent life-giving principle when it is separated from God. The process of spiritualization was related to the passage from an objective to a subjective interpretation of spirit. The objective interpretation was a naturalist one, whereas the subjective interpretation implied spiritualization— or, in other words, liberation from the original naturalism and materialism. In Philon man is already created in the Divine image through the agency of Divine inspiration. The human spirit is Divine; but the spirit in him rather than man himself is Divine. Philon identifies the Logos, Sophia and *pneuma*. Logos is the Divine spirit. Philon rebels against the Stoical materialist interpretation of spirit. He exalts the *pneuma*, attributing to it a religious character at the expense of the *nous*, which preserves its philosophical character. But, nevertheless, Philon's doctrine of spirit is rather Greek than Hebrew in origin. His *pneuma* and Logos coincide almost completely. The *pneuma* is not created, but divinely infused into man. The *pneuma*, like reason, is a Divine gift of grace. It is the source of the highest virtue. Philon transcends the limitations of Greek philosophy when he speaks of spirit as a Divine gift. But the best philosophy of the time maintained that God was Spirit, and in this way proved superior to the naturalistic Hebrew interpretation of the *pneuma*. In the complex history of the investigation into the nature of the spirit there was a variety of interpretations, religious and philosophical: philosophy generally conceived the spirit in terms of reason or mind; religious thought, on the other hand, conceived the spirit more integrally as an impulse of the higher life, as a force divinely infused into man. But at the same time the popular religious conceptions were still tainted with naturalism. The psychic *pneuma*

originated in the primordial helioistic interpretation of matter
which identified *pneuma* with air, fire or body; but, nevertheless,
this was an integral conception of life. The philosophical apprehension of the spirit surmounts the naturalistic, physical and
vitalist interpretations. But it lacks vital integrity, for it holds
reason to be superior to the whole life. In *nous* Greek philosophy
discovered another word to denote the spirit. Thus *pneuma* and
nous were synonyms for Philon, who was inclined to confuse
and identify his terms. But that does not apply to Greek thought
in general.

Greek philosophy on the whole preferred the term *nous* when
treating of spirit. But *nous* likewise connotes reason, intellect,
Logos. Greek philosophy affirms the intellectual principle as the
essential attribute of spirit. The intellectual principle is exalted
above the sensible world; it alone is spiritual and Divine. In the
French translation of Plotinus *nous* is rendered by *intelligence*.
This interpretation of spirit was inherited by the scholastics. Here
we are already far removed from the ancient interpretation of
pneuma as inspiration, breath. The earlier naturalism is overcome,
but its place is taken by objective reason. In Plato and Aristotle
spirit is the highest impulse of the soul, but it is primarily an
intellectual force. In Plotinus, for whom spirit is invariably *nous*,
the spirit-intellect is an emanation of the Divine One. Similarly,
in Scholasticism, in Thomism, spirit is always and uniquely an
intellectual force enabling man to establish contact with being.
But this is not yet the *ratio* of modern rationalistic philosophy.
For Plato the non-material world fails to be the spiritual world.
For him the spiritual world is a world of ideas apprehensible by
means of concepts, a world of stability. In general, the term *nous*
is associated with Platonic dualism and idealism, whereas the
term *pneuma* is associated with Stoicism, monism and helioistic
materialism. Thus *pneuma* is a vital force, whereas *nous* is reason,
the ethical principle. Man's divine content is *nous*. The spiritual
part of the human soul is emphasized in Plato. The *pneuma*, on

the other hand, has associations with a popular belief in demons and gods who control and inspire the human soul. But Platonism exalts man's highest spiritual principle to the level of a universal ideal world in which ideas reign supreme. This is, of course, primarily an intellectual principle. The achievement of Greek philosophy was to overcome man's dependence on the power of good or evil spirits, to subordinate him to the rule of reason and intellect. Later Greek philosophy interprets spirit as wisdom. The *pneuma* of the Stoics, like the Logos, is a universal principle partaking of both reason and body. Both matter ($\H{v}\lambda\eta$) and spirit are body ($\sigma\H{\omega}\mu\alpha$). The spiritual life is in harmony with the universal Logos immanent in the world. Plutarch's human spirit (*nous*) is the Divine principle, the Divine emanation; but the human soul is part of the universal soul. The premise of a cosmic spirit, of a cosmic Logos, was the stage beyond Platonic dualism. Actually, it involved a return to naturalism. Whereas Plato affirmed the spiritual character of reason, its relation to the world of ideas, the Stoics and the later Neo-Platonists endowed spirit again with a helioistic character. This is particularly evident in the Stoic doctrine of the spermatic Logos.

The concepts, *pneuma* and *nous*, are intricately related. As we have already noted, the *pneuma* is for Plato and Aristotle the lower, non-spiritual element. But while Philon spiritualized the *pneuma*, it becomes materialized again in Neo-Platonism. The interpretation of *nous*, on the other hand, is more constant and never assumes materialistic forms. Alexandrian philosophy established a distinction between the universal Logos on the one hand and human reason and external nature on the other. Plotinus, who is no longer a representative of classical Greece but who stands on the threshold of two worlds in an age of intense spiritual research, fused in his masterly system all the discoveries of previous Greek thought. His *nous*, the intellect, situated between the one and the many, succeeds in preserving its purity. Human evil appears to result from the mixture of the pure unifying part of human nature with the material plural world. The achievement of spirituality ensures a control of this mixture, a definition of man's eternally pure element. But Greek intellectualism survived in the Plotinian interpretation of the spirit. There is no magic in Plotinus's work such as haunted the other neo-Platonists like Iamblichus and Proclus. Greek spiritual life depended on man's harmony with the cosmos. Medieval spirituality was founded on man's harmony with God. But there are signs in Neo-Platonism that man's harmonious relations with the cosmos were already breaking down. Spirit was invading the confines of cosmic life. A syncretic tendency was apparent among the Gnostics; their *pneuma* was both physical and spiritual; and cosmic forces ruled the human spirit liberated by Christianity. Their spirit was fluid matter. Nevertheless, the Gnostics were extreme spiritualists. Hindu religious philosophy, on the other hand, is essentially spiritual and acosmic; its *manos* is both spirit and thought. The *Atman*, man's spiritual foundation, is identical with the *Brahman*. Hindu thought has an original greatness of its own; its categories differ from the Western categories of being and non-being. Being originates from non-being. The creation of the world is interpreted as a sacrifice of God. The world is the transformation of the First Cause. Hindu thought is more spiritualistic than Greek thought; it spiritualizes the spirit. In this sense, it has an affinity with Plotinus. It is really a form of spiritual monism. The Ego loses its identity in the Absolute Self, in the *Atman*. There is no personal spirit in the Hindu spirituality; the personal is general rather than individual. Christianity, however, introduced essentially new features into the interpretation of the spirit.

The conception of spirit revealed in the Gospel is a development of the biblical one, but in addition it represents a spiritualization involving a new revelation. Everything in the Gospel is governed by and through the spirit. We are no longer confronted with the philosophical *nous*, but with the *pneuma* of religious revelation. The *pneuma* of the New Testament is not human consciousness or thought, but a spiritual state determined by Divine inspiration. Spirit is the Holy Spirit, bearing the same relation to the soul as blood to the body. Spirit is always a protection, a help, a solace, an inspiration. But most remarkable of all, the only unpardonable sin is that against spirit; the sin against the Son, against Christ, is pardonable. This helps to show the great importance attached to spirit. The Gospel constantly holds out the promise of the spirit. Spirit is all-powerful; when inspired by It, man does everything through spirit. The Kingdom of God is revealed in spirit. The breath of spirit is made to account for every strong temporary derangement and unusual event. The Divine inspiration would appear to annihilate the human Ego. Spirit is invariably identified with power—an attribute lacking in the philosophical *nous*. In the Apostolic Church, spirit was no dogma or doctrine, but the fundamental fact of the religious life. The real, non-symbolic charism of early Christianity is related to spirit. The necessary distinction between the various kinds of spirit was also accomplished through the spirit. The opposition between *spirit* and *flesh* established by St. Paul was a fundamental one. This opposition is a strictly religious one, and has nothing in common with the philosophical antithesis of spirit and matter. St. Paul could not conceive of spirit existing independently of God and Christ; it was spirit that made men Christian. On the basis of the New Testament interpretation of spirit, Tareyev maintains that spirit, far from being the second or third component part of human nature, is in fact the Divine principle in man. In the Pauline context *flesh* is not synonymous with *body*; it is a religious category of sin rather than a natural-physical phenomenon. The spiritual struggle against the flesh is a struggle against sin. In this context flesh is no longer matter in the Greek philosophical or Plotinian sense. Nor is evil conceived as a mixture of the pure human element with baser matter. Until the coming of Jesus spirit was engaged in preparing the renascence of faith. In the view of the Church, however, the Spirit-Paraclete is the

exclusive property of the faithful, of the members of the Church.
But Jesus Christ appealed to the whole world, to the whole of
humanity. The Paracelete is only bestowed on a group of the
elect. The Second Coming of Christ is awaited as a gift of the
Holy Spirit. After the Ascension there remained in the world the
Holy Spirit, the Paraclete. St. John, the beloved apostle, finds
comfort and support in spirit. We are now confronted with a
very complex problem: Was spirit originally conceived as a
personality, was there a hypostasis of spirit? In St. John the spirit
is more personal than in St. Paul. The problem of spirit becomes
exclusively that of the Holy Spirit. But the doctriné of the Holy
Spirit remains the least explored and developed part of the Christian theology. For a long time the Holy Spirit was interpreted
subordinately. The Holy Spirit is Divine, but there was some
difficulty in acknowledging It as God, as a Hypostasis of the Holy
Trinity, together with the Hypostases of the Father and the Son.
This was no accident. The Holy Spirit is the nearest to and the
most immanent in man; the spiritual, the emanation of spirit,
becomes a human property, a component part of man; through
spirit a Divine element is infused into man. For this very reason,
spirit can least of all be represented as an object of rational and
objectified knowledge. We shall consider this point later in greater
detail. The theological doctrine of the Holy Spirit involves
irreconcilable contradictions. Patristic thought is of no great help
to pneumatology. The Holy Spirit is an agent whose nature is not
revealed. The doctors of the Church, who are permeated with
Neo-Platonism, attempt to propound a doctrine of the Holy
Spirit vitiated by Philosophical concepts and far removed from
the original teaching of the Holy Scripture. According to St.
Gregory of Nyssa, a most remarkable thinker, spirit is the conceptional part of man as distinct from his sensible soul and nutri-
tive body. Thus *pneuma* again becomes *nous*. Everything is
governed by reason and wisdom interpreted in the Greek sense.
In St. Augustine the soul becomes—perhaps for the first time—

a spiritual substance. In Tertullian the soul is still material. In St. Irenius spirit forsakes the sinful man, a conception more in keeping with the early evangelical and apostolic one. The scholastics, in their turn, attempt to reconcile Greek philosophy with Christian theology. But there is no sign of a lucid, established and consistent doctrine of spirit and the Holy Spirit. The writings of the saints transformed the Greek and Pagan conceptions of spirituality by stressing the fundamental importance of the heart as opposed to reason. In Karl Barth's dialectical theology, spirit reveals, manifests and realizes itself paradoxically and dialectically, without at the same time being incommensurable with man. Christianity introduces into its interpretation of spirit not only an intellectual but also an ethical moment. But spirit and spirituality remain essentially the property of mysticism, and are best of all revealed in mystical writings.

The distinction between the biblical, evangelical and apostolic interpretation of spirit on the one hand, and that of Greek philosophy on the other, is clearly manifest. In the former spirit is a blessed energy overflowing from another world into our own; in the latter spirit is an ideal foundation of the world, reason itself, towering above the sensible world. In both cases the *pneuma* is spiritualized and its primeval and physical associations transcended. European philosophical thought was on the whole to approximate more to the conceptions of Greek philosophy than to those of the Scripture. *Nous* is more familiar to philosophical thought than *pneuma*. Nevertheless Christianity radically transformed Greek intellectualism. German mysticism, which was to play an important part in the history of spirit, was the source of a new approach to the problem; and later German philosophy was to develop this more fully. It is, however, surprising that the concept of spirit should have been comparatively ignored by European philosophical thought, and that its essence should have remained undefined. The spirit was studied chiefly in the sphere of mysticism and religion. In Hegelian philosophy the spirit occupies a predominant place; but Greek intellectualism and the Greek Logos are so transformed therein that freedom, which was an alien notion to the Greeks, becomes the primary attribute of spirit. But Hegel interpreted freedom in a particular way. The philosophical spiritualization of the *pneuma*, its exaltation above cosmic life, takes place chiefly through a process of intellectual objectification. Spirit was conceived as objective being, as an established universal concept. This notion had a discouraging effect on the development of theology. German philosophy succeeded partially in overcoming this obstacle, at least in so far as it passed beyond naïve realism and objectivism. Naïve realism and logical universalism are, indeed, alien to the Christian revelation. In the Scripture, spirit, like the subjective spirit, is certainly neither objective nor universal. The objective interpretation of spirit was predominantly a philosophical tendency. Modern philosophy is largely rationalistic. It has no use for the intellect of Plotinus or that of St. Thomas Aquinas, its knowledge is limited to the *ratio*. Wolff, the German luminary, defines spirit as substance elaborated by reason and free will. That is an example of pedantic rationalism. Kant, who talks of spirit in a rationalistic enlightened way, has no philosophy of spirit in the true sense of the word. However, we should note his distinction involving spirit, between freedom and determined nature. Post-Kantian German philosophy considers freedom to be the chief attribute of spirit. Herder discovers in spirit the qualities of a concrete carrier of psychic-cultural primal forms. He is the first to speak of the spirit of a language, of a national spirit, and so on. He sets out to find the sources of spirit in the historical world. The Divine Spirit becomes immanent in the natural man. The Romantics revived the cosmic-naturalistic conception of spirit as an all-animating fluid. In Fichte, spirit is an aspiration towards the supernatural. Incidentally, Fichte hardly ever refers to 'spirit' in his earlier writings, and he treats of it only in his later period. Schelling's conception of spirit is related to his theory of identity.

Spirit is likened to a sort of immature nature, whereas nature itself is a mature spirit. But in his *Philosophie der Mythologie* he defines spirit otherwise: spirit is the self-possessing, the self-containing, the potential, the power in being. Schleiermacher uses the term spirit in a pantheistic sense. Spirit is the union of the Divine and human natures. He speaks of the spirit of a community. But Hegel is the most interesting of all, because he was the first to attempt to formulate a philosophy of spirit.

The most remarkable feature of the Hegelian doctrine of spirit is that no abyss of objectivity intervenes between man and God, between spirit and spirit. Spirit is *being-in-itself* and *being-for-itself* —that is to say, it does not constitute an object for the subject. Spirit is Logos; and thus an element of Greek intellectualism enters into the Hegelian interpretation of spirit. Nevertheless, freedom, its chief attribute, is of Christian origin. Being is freedom for and in itself. Actually, Hegel is a monist; he admits no human or Divine reason and spirit, but only one humanizing reason and spirit. Reason is the dwelling-place of spirit in which God is revealed. The highest perception of spirit is also self-knowledge. *Ich bin Kämpfende und der Kampf,* says Hegel. Religion is the self-knowledge of the Divine Spirit expressed through the concrete spirit or man. Hegel claims spiritual apprehension to be most concrete. The servants of philosophy are spiritual persons. Spirit is revealed only to the spirit, God's utterance is uniquely spiritual. Religion is the relationship of one spirit to another. Both religion and philosophy exist only by virtue of the fact that man is spirit. Spirit is an idea which has realized itself in being. Therefore freedom is the essence of spirit. But in the case of man spirit has a general rather than a particular connotation. This is the Platonic intellectualist rather than the Christian side of Hegelian philosophy. Hegel is a universalist who fails to apprehend the mystery of the personality and of the relationship of one personal spirit to another. Spirit as a form of relation to one's self is a subjective spirit. On the other hand, spirit is objective when it assumes the form of a real world in which freedom is necessity. Spirit is soul, consciousness, subject. The soul is a concept, formed by means of it. Spirit is the truth of matter. The Ego is the relationship of spirit to itself, to the subjective. Truth, like reason, is the identity of the subjective and the objective-universal aspects of the concept. Spirit is a consciousness of self as an infinite universality. Feeling is particularistic, whereas thought alone is universal. Spirit is an identity of the subjective and the objective. The ethical power is the perfection of the absolute spirit. The relationship between lordship and slavery is resolved in the spirit. Hegelian philosophy aspires to be an esoteric revelation of God. While Hegel maintained that freedom was the cardinal attribute of spirit, Fichte discovered it in human creative activity. But Fichte's active Ego is pure subjectivity rather than individuality. There is no personality, no personal spirit, but merely a subjective spirit in both Hegel and Fichte. Fichte regards nature as a sort of dead freedom, as a pure past. Fichte's real contribution was his conception of spirit as creative activity. By virtue of this he approximates more nearly to the truth than Hegel. But Hegel was the first to broach a whole philosophy of spirit. His system arrives at a synthesis of Greek intellectualist universalism and the Christian interpretation of spirit as freedom and dynamism. But the weakness of Hegelian philosophy lay in its failure to grasp the inner essence of the personality, of personal spirituality, of the personal relationship between man and God. Thus Hegel failed to establish a concrete philosophy of spirit or to escape from the sphere of abstract universality. Although he transcends pre-Kantian objectivism, he persists in affirming the doctrine of the objective spirit despite the fact that his original premise will not admit the intervention of the object between spirit and spirit. Finally, the evolutionary or determinist principle also vitiates the Hegelian conception of spirit, and, in fact, contradicts the notion of spirit as freedom. The Hegelian philosophy of spirit is a secularized version of

c

German mysticism, adapted to the needs of the nineteenth century consciousness; and, of course, it reflects the monophysite bias of that mysticism. But German mysticism had also introduced that *Innerlichkeit*, that original spirituality, which has become an essential part of German philosophy as a whole.

After Hegel, we owe the most interesting attempt to found a systematic philosophy of spirit to N. Hartmann, in his work *Das Problem des Geistigen Seins*. More recently, Gentile's *Esprit Acte Pure* develops the thought of Fichte and Hegel; but it is more concerned with the foundations of a philosophical system on the basis of an active spirit than with the immediate problem of spirit. Gentile has, however, contributed a distinction between spirit and nature, and an active-dynamic interpretation of the spirit. His investigations are on the whole confined to the sphere of German Idealism. Hartmann approaches the problem of spirit in a very subtle way. His chief deficiency consists in the little use he makes of religious and mystical experience. Like Hegel, he conceives spirit as *being-for-itself*. He establishes a distinction between spirit and consciousness. Consciousness is not one of the characteristics of spirit, for spirit unites whereas consciousness isolates. In his opinion, consciousness is not transferable. He agrees with Scheler in repudiating decisively the vitalistic conception of spirit as an epiphenomenon of life. The lowest categories associated with spiritual being are the weakest. But the impotence of the highest categories is a source of human strength, of human freedom. The spiritual sphere is one of struggle, postulating freedom. Spirit has the power of revealing a purpose; it is expansive. The relationship between the general and the particular spirit can never be conceived in the light of a relationship between substance and accident. Spirit gains its spatial experience through the body. But the spiritual life is always freer from the determined than from the corporeal life. Acts are the means by which the personality transcends itself. It might be argued that spirit is a means by which being ascends. But the core of Hartmann's philosophy demonstrates that his conception of spirit is poised in the void. Spirit is the ontic ultimate, not situated in spiritual being; but nevertheless, supreme. Although conditioned by material existence, spirit is the supreme value. Hartmann does not associate spirit with God. His philosophy of spirit is atheistic; it becomes, in fact, a philosophy of ideal values beyond which no being transpires. Spirit has no proper existence of its own. More interesting, perhaps, are Hartmann's ideas about the objectification of spirit. The objective spirit, as he sees it, lacks both consciousness and personality. Communities, such as a nation, are realities, but not personalities, subjects or consciousnesses. The objective spirit has no being. Hence the deduction should be made that there is no objective spirit, but only an objectification of spirit. There is this to be said for Hartmann—that, although his philosophy is not existential, he did make spirit the object of his investigations. Very few references can be found to the spirit in the works of other philosophers. Windelband and Dilthey interpret spirit in relation to the idea of value, deriving this conception from Lotze. Spiritual values are revealed in historical existence. Bergson identifies spirit with pure memory. But Bergsonian philosophy is vitalistic, and it cannot therefore postulate an independent spirit. Scheler's spirit, although clearly distinguished from life, is passive. Cohen and Brunschvicg interpret spirit from a strictly rationalistic standpoint. For them the source of spirit lies in pure thought. According to Brunschvicg mathematics and spirit are one and the same. In Jaspers' philosophy spirit is essentially that towards which human transcendence is directed. Man is constantly investigating his consciousness, meeting obstacles and then always transcending them. For Jaspers the metaphysical is a symbol, by means of which existence scrutinizes the depths of being. The consciousness becomes a seer by deciphering symbols. Man is made complete only through transcendence. Jaspers' is symbolist philosophy of spirit. In place of ontological being Jaspers has cyphers and symbols. Thus Jaspers' existential philosophy attempts to transcend conceptional ontology. Incidentally, it is interesting to note that dialectical materialism goes back to the pre-Philonist material-istic, physical interpretation of the *pneuma*. This is by no means a final repudiation of spirit—an impossible task indeed—but it is an interpretation of it in terms of physical energy. It is, in fact, a return to the primeval helioistic conception of spirit. But, as we have observed, spiritualization has been the general trend in re-ligious experience as well as in philosophical thought. This process is by no means at an end. A new movement of the spirit is im-minent and will help to enlighten still further our conception of it. The whole experience of humanity, of its higher life, testifies to the reality of spirit. To deny this reality is to be blind to realities, to be unable to distinguish the qualities of being, or to describe what is thus distinguished. The reality of spirit is quite different from that of the natural world. This reality is not demon-strated, but is revealed by those able to distinguish qualities. The reality of spirit is independent of the categories of thought which leave their imprint on being. It would be an error to identify spirit and being. Spirit is freedom, creativeness. Spirit exercises a primacy over being, the primacy of freedom. An ontologically orientated *Weltanschauung* is static, whereas a pneumatologically orientated one is dynamic. Existential philosophy is not an ontological philosophy in the traditional sense of the word.

CHAPTER II

THE ATTRIBUTES OF SPIRIT

I

A rationalistic definition of spirit would not only be a presumptuous but also a hopeless undertaking. Such a definition would kill spirit or transmute it into object. Spirit defies conceptional interpretation, but nevertheless its attributes are apprehensible. Among these attributes are freedom, meaning, creativity, integrity, love, value, an orientation towards the highest Divine world and union with it. The *pneuma* of Scripture and the *nous* of Greek philosophy are included among these attributes. Since spirit is freedom, independence from natural or social determination would appear to be the primary attribute of the spiritual. Spirit is first of all opposed to any sort of determinism. Spirit is inward in contradistinction to anything external or anything conditioned by external causation. Inwardness is the symbol of spirit. The spatial symbols of depth and height may also serve to denote spirit. Spirit is both fathomless depth and heavenly height. It would be wrong to take away all activity from spirit, as Scheler does, and attribute it exclusively to life. The contrary is true, for spirit is active while life is passive in the biological sense of the word. But Scheler does fully understand that spirit is not an epiphenomenon of the life-process, that a vitalistic interpretation of it is inadequate. In this inert world spirit is energy, dynamism, creativeness, transcendence. Pico della Mirandola claims a heavenly or extra-natural origin for the human spirit. Hence spirit is an energy in the natural world rather than something determined by it. Through spirit man becomes a Divine image and likeness. Spirit is the Divine element in man; and through it man can ascend to the highest spheres of the Godhead. Spirit is man's

33

whole creative act. Spirit is freedom; and freedom has its roots
in the depths of pre-existential being. Freedom exercises a primacy
over being which is already a state of inert freedom. Hence spirit
cannot be defined in terms of a finite, completely formed and
more or less static being. Therefore spirit is creativeness—a creation of new being. The creative activity and freedom of the
subject are primal. The principle of causality is inapplicable to
spirit and the spiritual life. Spirit emanates from and is reabsorbed
by the Divine Essence. Through spirit man receives everything
from the Deity and through it he gives back everything to the
Deity, magnifying the gifts bestowed on him and creating the
hitherto non-existent. Spirit emanates from God but it is not a
Divine creation like nature; it is a Divine infusion, an inspiration.
That is the biblical image. But spirit emanates not only from the
Deity but also from the primal pre-existential freedom, from the
Ungrund. That is, indeed, the fundamental paradox of spirit: it is
a Divine emanation, and at the same time it can reply to the Deity
in terms not dictated by It. Spirit is not only Divine, it is also
divinely human, Divine wordly; it is freedom in God and from
God. No concept or rationalization is adequate to express this
mystery; only myth and symbol can attempt to do so. This is the
mystery of creation, and, at the same time, that of evil. Man regarded as a natural determined creature is not aware of this
mystery; such an awareness is the sign of a spiritual creature.
Freedom, creativeness and evil postulate not only being but also
non-being. But this non-being, this nothingness, escapes objectification or the attempts of conceptional thought to grasp it. It
would be wrong to say that non-being is or exists. It can be said,
however, that it has an existential purpose—a significance in the
destines of man and of the world. The Logos is akin to spirit, it
informs everything with purpose. But at the same time spirit is
irrational, extra-rational, supra-rational. The rationalistic interpretation of spirit only deforms and debases it. When confronted
with man's irrational, unconscious nature, spirit struggles bravely

to dominate it. In this process of spiritualization—not rationalization—my natural foundations appear alien and determined from
without. Nature is external whereas spirit is inward. Spirit is the
only means of understanding both God and man. Spirit human-
izes man's conception of God and, at the same time, liberates him
from crude anthropomorphism. Spiritualistic theosophy is essentially *apophatic*. Spirit is always a reality orientated towards eternity. Spirit is timeless as well as spaceless. Spirit is whole and
resists division in time or space. Spirit is not being, but the purpose and truth of being. Spirit is mind, the whole mind, Spirit is
both transcendent and immanent. The transcendental and the immanent become fused in spirit. Spirit is not the same thing as
consciousness, but consciousness is formed through spirit and
through it, again, reaches superconsciousness. There is a Promethean principle in spirit, a rebellion against the natural gods,
against the determinism of human destiny, an aspiration to a
higher, freer world.

Spirit is a quality rising above any principle of mundane utility,
any use of doubtful means, any external achievements and realizations, any instruments of worldly power, any public opinion,
any social exigencies. Spirit is everywhere and in everything active
as an illuminating, transfiguring and liberating force. Spirit is an
emancipating force from the power of the elements, that of earth
and blood, that of the cosmic-tellurgical forces which it dominates
but does not destroy. The process of spiritualization liberated man
from the power of magic, from magical forces and associations.
Initially spirit was almost indistinguishable from the natural
elements and was identified with magic. But magic is determinism, spirit is freedom. It would be an error, however, to
assume that civilized or cultured man has altogether escaped from
the power of magic, from the determinism exercised on his
destiny by cosmic-tellurgical forces. The primal elements are constantly surging up again and impeding the progress of spirit and
spirituality. The struggle for the spiritual kingdom is always being

waged, and will continue to be waged till the end of time. It is paradoxical that, although civilized man has ceased to understand the mysteries of cosmic life and has lost the ability to commune with them, cosmic and tellurgical forces still persist in man and assail his spirituality. A higher degree of spirituality would enable man to commune once more with the mysteries of cosmic life without having to submit to the determinism of its forces.

Bachofen made a remarkable discovery when he unearthed the ancient primeval layer of man's religious life, the religion of motherhood and earth, associated with matriarchy and primordial communism, with the reign of the chthonic gods. The spiritual awakening, that of the personal principle, implied a struggle of the solar masculine principle against the tellurgic feminine principle. It was a process of spiritualization. It would be an error to assume that this struggle is at an end, for it persists in a variety of new forms. In this context, spirit should not be regarded as a reality of the same kind as the cosmic-tellurgic forces, a reality supplanting and annihilating them. Spirit is, rather, a reality postulating an awareness of supreme quality, of the highest purpose latent in the cosmic-tellurgic forces. Klages among others deduces from Bachofen certain conclusions hostile to spirit; but Bachofen himself had an excellent comprehension of spirit as the highest principle, personal and solar, of liberation from the determinism of tellurgic and lunar forces. Spirit is a higher principle than life, just as freedom is a higher principle than determinism, the personality than impersonal elements, energy than passivity, integral purpose than purposelessness and diffuseness. But spirit is an active force in life and we should be able to distinguish its attributes in the vital process. The abstract spiritualism developed by several types of spiritual life and of philosophical systems seriously impeded the apprehension of the essential nature of spirit and of its attributes. Spirit was interpreted as an abstraction of the renouncement of the world, as a reality opposed to the realities of the world, whereas spirit is, on the contrary, an energy at work within all the realities of the world. It is, in fact, a higher concrete reality,—a whole, indivisible and inalienable. St. Thomas Aquinas had evidently this in mind when he stated that grace transfigured rather than repudiated nature. The spiritual world is not the natural world, but a supremacy over it. The natural world is ruled by determinist and impersonal forces, and its purpose is obscure; in the spiritual world, on the other hand, freedom reigns supreme on the foundations of personality and personal relationships, and the purpose of existence is clear. It is a victory over fallen nature, a symbol of cosmic liberation and illumination rather than of its denial and annihilation. Spirit is a sign that man is no slave but a master of cosmic forces, a friendly master and liberator. In this connection we must consider the part played by technical development and its inherent contradiction, spiritual in origin but anti-spiritual in effect. The organic conception of spirit put forward by the Romantics is a vitalistic one, since it associates spirit with the life-process. We shall have occasion hereafter to discuss the relation between technical development and the organism.

In the ordinary way, the term spirit is applied in a very wide and all-embracing sense. In the first place, spirit is used to denote all kinds of collectives. We speak of the spirit of a people, a class, a profession, an army, a family. We speak of the spirit of an age. We speak even of the spirit of materialism—of that which denies spirit. We speak, too, of the spirit of Capitalism which is itself the death of spirit. In this all-embracing and metaphorical sense, the term spirit loses its specific meaning. It almost becomes a 'characteristic', a clue to an identity. If freedom is the essential attribute of spirit, then this attribute is wanting in the collective spirit. We likewise speak of the spirit of evil. Are we to understand that the attributes of spirituality are discernible in the spirit of evil? The spirits of the angelic and the demoniac hierarchies are not personalistic in the sense in which the human world and God are personalistic. The natural spirits are also lacking in spiritual qualities.

Thus, spirituality is a liberation from the tyranny of the natural spirits. The spirit of any given class, army, family, *Weltanschauung*, can very well be a negation of spirituality. In this sense, spirit means little more than the energy uniting and consolidating a given group—an energy which may, indeed, be profoundly anti-spiritual. Thus the use of the category spirit in relation to collective groups of any kind is highly ambiguous and to be guarded against. Spirit has an *axiological* significance lacking in collectives. In the strict sense of the word, we should speak only of the personal and subjective spirit. The term *objective spirit* is already problematic, for an objective spirit can have no inner existence. Nor are collectives in any sense personalities. Nation, state, society, are individualities, stages in the individualization of life, but not personalities. The same is true of the Church, which is a reality but not a personality. Spirit is active in the Church but the Church itself is not a collective spirit. *Sobornost* is quite another matter; it is not a collective but a quality of community among men, among personalities and the We, a quality inherent in those personalities rather than one determining them from without in the form of a collective. The *Sobornost* We is immanent in men; it implies an ascending spirituality in them, a realization by them of a spiritual plane of being. In Christian dogma the Holy Spirit is conceived as a Hypostasis or a Person. The Holy Spirit is certainly not a collective Person, but to call It a Person at all is a way of symbolizing an inexplicable mystery—that of resolving the opposition between the personal and the universal. Spirit can be incarnated and symbolized but it never becomes objective.

II

In the history of spiritual consciousness the error has often been perpetrated of identifying spirit and soul, the spiritual and the psychic. It is a well-known problem of the spiritual life how to distinguish spiritual from psychic states. In all probability no one altogether escapes from this confusion. Spirituality is the highest quality we can discern in our judgment of men. Every man has a soul—such is his nature—but his spirituality may remain undiscovered or suppressed. Spirit is the highest quality of the soul, a symbol of freedom from the power of the world. Spirit is truth, the purpose of the soul. Philosophies, which fail to apprehend spirit in the same way as religious consciousness and mystical experience, do nevertheless distinguish spirit and term those values ideal which should be realized in human life. Spirit is *axiological*; it is not nature, not even psychic nature, but truth, beauty, purpose, freedom. The philosophy of ideal values is, of course, an imperfect philosophy of spirit, a philosophy poised in the void but one that still feels the necessity to detect some of the attributes of spirit. Spirit introduces the qualities of wholeness, unity and design into man's psychic and psychic-corporeal life. The soul is invariably fragmentary and partial; spirit alone is whole and universal. Spirit resolves the opposition between the particular and the universal, the personal and the supra-personal. The concrete man is a blending of the whole and the part. Only spirit can impart a concrete universal content to the personality and exalt it above its spatial and temporal limitations. Without the spiritual principle the soul is hermetic. A philosophy of spirit should teach universalistic personalism at the expense of particularistic individualism. The antithesis, spirit or flesh, is an error. The antithesis is only conceivable when *flesh* is regarded as sin rather than as a natural part of the human constitution. The Cartesian dualism of spirit and body is entirely wrong, and has since been superseded in contemporary philosophy and psychology. Man is a whole creature, an organism compounded of spirit, soul and body. The body is an integral part of the human personality, image and likeness. The human image is the supreme achievement of cosmic life, a victory over chaos. *Spirituality* is not opposed to *body* or *material* but implies its transfiguration, the realization of the highest quality of the whole man—his personality. This realiza-

tion is achieved through a victory of spirit over the chaotic elements of soul and body. Spirit is the masculine active principle
whereas the soul is the feminine passive principle. Spirit comes
from the Logos, while the soul is cosmic. Spirit performs an act
in relation to the soul; it informs it with purpose and truth, it
liberates it from the power of cosmic forces. This does not imply
that spirit crushes or supplants the human soul. There has, indeed,
been such a conception of spirit and spirituality, but it was essentially anti-human. The soul is the kernel of the human creature
and the function of spirit should be to endow the soul with the
highest quality and purpose. Spiritual life is a spiritual-psychic
life. A purely spiritual love divorced from the soul is a perverted,
impersonal and inhuman love. It contradicts the divinely human
conception of love propounded in the Gospel. Thus in Plotinus,
for example, there is a separation of the pure intellectual element
in man from matter: the first realizes the One, the second is not
transfigured. This is a negation of the *whole* personality.

In many of the spiritualistic writings of the ascetics there is a
false non-Gospel interpretation of love and the spiritual life. This
tendency, though in a different context, is also common to German Idealism. A philosophy of this kind tends to sacrifice the
human soul to the Absolute Spirit. It is a sacrifice of the personality and humanity. It is a philosophy of abstract spirit. And man,
living concrete man, must rebel against such an interpretation of
spirit. In Feuerbach's reaction against this conception there was a
sane element, a reminder that man, whom Hegel had overlooked,
still existed. In his doctrine of the Categorical Imperative and the
pure moral will Kant had already embarked upon the path of
denying the soul, the living concrete man. Thus an ideal norm,
an ideal value, becomes a means of suppressing man and his
emotional life. The spiritual life is truth, but it is also the life of
man, of the whole man. The elimination of the human element
in the name of either an ascetic war against sin or some ideal
value is equally perverse, false and sinful. Of all things, the hardest

and most paradoxical to comprehend is the relation between spirit and personality, the universal content communicated by spirit to man himself with his complex emotional life and unique personal destiny. The universality of spirit does not imply a tyranny of the general, abstract, all-human, impersonal over the individual. The universality of spirit does help, in fact, to make the entity of the personality concrete. In St. Thomas Aquinas form (*spirit*) is universal while individualization is a material process. This is an erroneous interpretation of the relation between spirit and personality. Spirit is universalistic and personalistic. It is the Divine element in man, but it is inseparable from the human element and acts in conjunction with it. That is the mystery of Divine humanity. There are various influences at work in disintegrating this whole divinely human spiritual life. In Greek thoughts, in Plotinus, in idealist philosophy, the spiritually interpreted intellectual element tends to supplant the cordial, the psychic-emotional element; in ascetic and mystical writings, on the other hand, the intellectual element is frequently related to the soul and then eliminated. The temptation to violate the spiritual, divinely human whole is ever present. Man is reluctant to admit the notion of plenitude. But in Eastern Christianity there is a special comprehension of the heart as the kernel of the human creature and his spiritual life. In the light of this conception the heart appears not as man's emotional-psychic nature but as a spiritual-psychic whole comprising also a transfigured mind. Man's longing for truth and purpose, for spirituality, is an essential part of his nature; it is not deducible from the psychic and vitalistic process but emanates directly from the Divine spirit inherent in man. Inspired by Bachofen and Nietzsche, Klages opposed spirit to life, spirit to soul. He differed from Bachofen in that he considered spirit—for him identical with reason, intellect, consciousness—as a parasite inimical to life. Spirit is a diseased, life-fettering product of the vital process. Klages affirmed that the mysteries had been able to liberate the soul from spirit. The liberated soul, emancipated from spirit, from the tyrannical intellectual principle, appeared as a sort of paradise regained. Such is the interpretation of spirit propounded by the so-called philosophy of life (*Lebensphilosophie*). Klages's conception is significant only as a reaction against rationalism. It fails to grasp the fact that spirit is primarily freedom. Leon Shestov is also an enemy of spirit which he identifies with reason and morality—in other words, with necessity.

The abstract interpretation of spirit common to intellectuals, who as a class are denied the full life, is the result of a false dualism of spirit and flesh, of spiritual and intellectual work on the one hand, and material and physical labour on the other. It is the classic heritage of aristocratic Greek intellectualism. Christianity has brought about a change in this respect, but the traditional Christian spirituality is hostile to life in the world. In modern times there has been an increasing tendency to favour a marked dualism of spiritual and physical labour on the basis of the intellectualist interpretation of spirituality. The creative intellectuals form groups and live according to their own laws. Spirituality is understood hermetically, in a literary way, in terms of an academy. In the Middle Ages spiritual life was centred in the monasteries, which postulated a greater degree of integrity. But the problem of labour, considered in all its stages as a spiritual problem, was not propounded till the nineteenth century, when, in a period of decaying spirituality, it was clearly stated by Marx. This problem is closely associated with the necessity of a new spirituality in the world. Spirituality affects the whole of life, the whole of man—his body as well as his physical labour. It would be an error to assume that physical labour could be relegated to a special sphere distinct from the spiritual one. It would likewise be an error to assume that technical development, which is so important a part of modern life, could be divorced from spirituality. This error is the great evil and falsehood of the bourgeois world. It accounts for the fictitiousness of bourgeois life. A state of mechanized and materialized human labour is a sinful and fallen one. Spiritual force is required of inventors but not of employers, of those who merely exploit technical achievements. The lowest forms of material labour demand a certain spiritual effort on the part of man. Now spirit is the force revealing itself in the complete life. In this sense, the endeavour to humanize labour is a process of spiritualization. Man's mastery of technical means is a spiritual achievement, a spiritualization of technical development itself. The notion of a whole humanity postulates the resolution of a false dualism, the incarnation of spirit, the spiritualization of the flesh and of all forms of labour. Integral humanity will prove to be the new spirituality animating the whole of life and human labour. This notion is implicit in Christianity but was not properly elaborated in the traditional, spiritualistic philosophies. A false and illusory spirituality was born of the separation of the spiritual from the whole life. This illusory, hallucinating communion with spirits and the spirit world is the outstanding feature of certain types of occult philosophies, of theosophy and spiritualism. They are all the result of the violence done to human integrity.

The terms subjective and objective spirit, personal and universal spirit, have a general currency. In using these terms primacy is usually accorded to the objective over the subjective spirit, to the universal over the personal spirit. This is the natural consequence of postulating the primordiality of the universals, the primacy of the genus over the individual. In this context the subjective and personal spirit is usually interpreted psychologically, whereas the objective and universal spirit is interpreted ontologically. Actually, the very term *objective spirit* is highly problematic and ambiguous. In becoming an object, anything objective can be said to have no inner existence. An inner existence is the privilege of the subject, the Ego, the Thou and the We. The reality of the We cannot be objective. There is no such thing as objective spirit, but there is objectified spirit. It follows that spirit is always personal and related to the personality. Freedom, creative activity, wholeness, loving communion with God and with men, are all the exclusive property of the subject and the personality. A hypostasis of the objective spirit is inconceivable. In objective spirit there can be no communion with God, no love, no freedom, no fathomless impulse. It is essentially determinist and legalistic, it is a concept mistakenly identified with an independent reality. There is a concrete universality distinct from an abstract generality. This concrete universality is not extra-personal, but is the highest content of the personal life, the sum of the personality's supra-personal values. God is a Person rather than a Universal Essence. The agency of the Divine Spirit on the human spirit is not a sign of the objective and universal spirit, but a resolution of the opposition between the personal and universal, the subjective and the so-called objective. Such is the mysterious agency of the Divine Spirit in the human world. The notion of *Sobornost* is related to this. The collective or objective spirit determines the personal spiritual life from without. But spirit is freedom, neither determining nor determined. The collective spirit is merely a metaphorical expression concealing the socialization of spirit in human life. The agency of the *Sobornost* spirit and that of social determinism on man are diametrically opposed. The socialization of spirit engenders the illusion of consciousness. Spirit is opposed to the social, objectified aspect of religion. Hartmann establishes a distinction between the objective and the collective spirit. But this distinction rests on the acceptance of objective spirit, of the Hegelian concept. Actually, the objective spirit is merely a state of human consciousness and spirituality, a state reminiscent of the Hegelian 'unhappy consciousness'. The objective spirit is related to the *credo* of the majority, to the category of number. Spirit is *being-in-itself* and the transcendence of spiritual life is not a process of exteriorization. There is no objective spirit but merely objectified spirit, no collective spirit but merely a socialized spirit. This exteriorization of spirit is but an inner moment in spiritual growth, it is merely a spiritual state. This brings us to the problem of the relation between spirit and history.

Spirit and history are closely interrelated. It could be argued that spirit is historical, that spirit alone apprehends history. That is what Hartmann believed, and he gave his work on spiritual existence the subtitle, *The foundations of the philosophy of history*. Dilthey explored history for the evidence of the existence of spirit. In Hegel, history is the self-revelation of spirit. History is particularly closely associated with spirit in the Christian consciousness. Unlike the Greek philosophers, Christian thinkers conceived spirit historically. The agency of freedom is peculiar to the sphere of history, it is unknown in the sphere of nature. History is our particular world more than nature. But nevertheless man fails to apprehend his own subjective spirit, his own spiritual freedom, in history. Instead, there is an abstraction of man's subjective spirit in the historical sphere. History above all raises the problem of the existence of an objective universal spirit. History may be considered in two aspects. On the one hand, history is our human affair and we detect in it the attributes of our own deeper nature, of spirit. History is with us and in us, and we can discover it in the depths of spirit. But on the other hand, history operates a divorce between our nature and our spirit. History becomes a fatality, an independent and ruthless force opposed to our freedom. According to Hegel, history is the self-revelation and development of freedom; but that freedom is independent of ours, it is not for us. Thus history realizes non-human ends, those of a cunning universal reason and spirit. History excludes the human personality. Our human spirituality becomes a refuge from history, from its cruel, ruthless and anti-human purpose. Spirit is incarnated in history, in historic epochs and civilizations, in the objective values of culture. But its various incarnations are not comparable to the flame and freedom of spirit as revealed in the subject. History is not only a spiritual incarnation but also a sign of spiritual failure, a confession that

D

the Kingdom of God is no nearer realization. The affirmation of the immanency of God and spirit in history leads to essentially conservative results. But spirit is revolutionary. The historical incarnation of spirit gives rise to the conservative force of inertia. Spirit ceases to exist in itself or for itself, it becomes exterior existence; in other words, it loses its chief attribute—freedom. This is in no sense transcendence, an ascent rather than a descent. Thus an historical objectification of spirit is a failure to realize the Kingdom of God.

Spirit implies an intermittent dynamism in the life and history of the world. The agency of spirit is not evolutionary. There is no consistent development of spirit, for this would imply a law and would be a negation of freedom. Hegelian freedom was such a law. Spirit is a dynamic force transcending frontiers and limitations. The transcendental is mysterious and infinite. This mystery and infinity give rise to spirit. Its agency is immanent in man, spiritual experience is immanent in him. But this is a transcendental rather than an immanent immanence. Spirit is a constant transcending of human life. There is essentially no such thing as a static transcendental but only the act of transcending. This is part of the mystery of spirit and the spiritual life. Spirit is *being-in-itself* or being not determined from without. But at the same time the life of spirit is a ceaseless transcending of limitations, an impulse of freedom rather than of determination. Purely natural processes are immanent, they are confined within the narrow limits of determinism. Spiritual processes, on the other hand, are transcendental because they are founded on freedom. But the transcendental and the immanent are correlative. Spirit is existence in one's own proper world; therein the transcendental is one's own property. God is transcendental; an abyss separates man from Him. But the transcendental nature of God is our immanent experience. Divinity is revealed in man, it is an inner human reality. That is another proof of the free agency of the Divine. God is not object, nor is spirit; objectified being is merely an objectifying process in the development of being. Hence there is no determination from without. Everything spiritual is subject, inward. There can be no spiritual emanation from the object. The spiritual has no significance other than freedom. Objectification is a secondary and derivative process, it should be grasped from within. In view of this, it is essential to understand the process of symbolism, the relation between symbol and reality.

CHAPTER III

THE OBJECTIFICATION OF SPIRIT
SYMBOLIZATION AND REALIZATION

I

As we have established, spirit is subject and is revealed in the subject.[1] But from without, spirit is objectified, exteriorized, outwardly formulated. Spirit manifests itself socially, it becomes socialized. Spirit expresses itself historically and becomes transformed in history, losing many of its attributes and assuming new ones. Spirit is inward, and that spatial symbol is one of its attributes. Everything spiritual emanates from within, from the inner depths. But this inwardness comes to be exteriorized. Spirit is *being-in-itself*, but in active formulation it inevitably becomes *being-for-another*. Thought must inevitably be expressed, but it is also true that *expressed thought* is in a certain sense falsehood. By its activity spirit is expansive. Spirit cannot help exteriorizing itself in another, in the world. It penetrates into a world which is not uniquely spiritual. And for spirit that is the origin of the tragedy. The plot of this tragedy is determined by the fact that spirit can neither remain a *being-in-itself* nor can it realize the sphere of objective spirit, since no such spirit exists but only spiritual objectification. In the process of objectification the subjective spirit loses its identity. The objectified spirit does not commune with a Thou or another spirit, but identifies itself with an object or the objective non-existential world; and in this case the subjective spirit concealed beyond it is its only link with existence. When the subjective spirit manifests itself in the

[1] The sense of the terms subject and object, subjective and objective has frequently changed in the history of philosophy. These terms have quite a different significance in Scholastic philosophy than in modern philosophy.

objective world, then spirit is abstracted from itself, and lost in objectivity.

Feuerbach maintained that a belief in God was nothing more than an abstraction of human nature, a projection of it into the transcendental sphere. Marx applied this notion to economics, and in particular to the economics of Capitalist society, in which he perceived an abstraction of the worker's human nature and labour, its transmutation into the material world of economics. This abstraction is the source of many illusions of consciousness. Both Feuerbach and Marx wished to restore man's abstracted nature to its original plenitude, but they failed to achieve this result because their vision of man was uniquely that of a material, non-spiritual, despoiled creature. The objectification of spirit in the historical world, in civilization, can be interpreted as an abstraction of man's spiritual nature. Thus man mistakes concepts, the elaborations of the creative and subjective spirit, for objective spiritual realities. A potential infinity, an infinite aspiration, is the peculiar characteristic of the subjective spirit or spirit in general. But objectification implies finality; the objective spirit is finite whereas the subjective spirit is infinite. The Greeks exalted the finite above the infinite; their vision was largely objective and founded on a spirit-cosmos and a spirit-world of ideas. As revealed in Christianity the subjective spirit is freedom.

Although Hartmann's premises are very different from mine, I find his ideas about the objective and objectified spirit very stimulating. He distinguishes between *objective* and *objectified*; he carries his distinction even further by distinguishing between *objectification* and *objection*: the first being active, the latter passive. I should have said that the objectification of spirit is proof of the agency of the subjective spirit, the result of the personal spirit's confrontation with a divided world, of the necessity it feels to commune with what is outside itself. But as it happens, the results of this process are interpreted as real objects which the subject is compelled to accept passively. In Hartmann the *objective* spirit is the motor of history, whereas the *objectified* spirit is orientated towards the ideal and eternal. This definition is hardly helpful. But in spite of his error in introducing the *objectified* spirit in this context, Hartmann does show a grasp of the conflict between the living and the objectified spirit. He is also aware of the process by which the living spirit is arrested. He even ventures to call the living spirit revolutionary and the objectified spirit tyrannical. The objectified spirit is conservative, and it is inevitably reabsorbed into the living spirit. The living spirit is a subjective personal spirit. In my own terminology I should formulate the problem thus: *Objectification, creating the illusion of an objective spirit subordinating spirit to law, puts an end to infinity.* Objectification is also the socialization of spirit, its ultimate subjection to everyday sociality. This socialization of spirit, this conservative finite principle, is manifest even in the history of revolutions. The objectification of spirit produces the bourgeois state (in the spiritual sense) and thus leads to the exhaustion of creative vital energy and activity. Objectification also inevitably breeds fiction, generally accepted as a socially useful instrument. All social activities depend on fictions of this kind. The pathos of pure truth remains essentially an affair of the subjective spirit. The fettering of spirit by everyday sociality is apparent in the organized activities of the State, the Church, academies, classes, the family, as well as in dogma as a system of rational concepts, conventions, customs, laws and norms. In contrast to all this we have the subjective flame of the personal spirit. The religious Socialist, L. Rogatz, expressed the hope that the proletariat, which had not so far been associated with property or involved in the decay of established values, would finally accept the heritage of infinity. This is an interesting but as yet unjustified idea, for the proletariat will also have to submit to a process of bourgeois objectification which will mean the end of infinity. Every victory in the sphere of cultural creativeness or social life implies objectification, a triumph of the objective over the subjective, of the general or the social over the personal. Spirit, like flame, like freedom, like creativeness, is opposed to any social stagnation or any lifeless tradition. In terms of Kantian philosophy—terms which I consider erroneous and confusing—spirit appears as a *thing-in-itself* and objectification as a *phenomenon*. Another and truer definition would be, spirit is *freedom* and objectification is *nature* (not in the romantic sense). Objectification has two aspects: on the one hand it denotes the fallen, divided and servile world, in which the existential subjects, the personalities, are materialized. On the other it comprehends the agency of the personal subject, of spirit tending to reinforce ties and communications in this fallen world. Hence objectification is related to the problem of culture, and in this consists the whole complexity of the problem.

In objectification there are no primal realities, but only symbols. The objective spirit is merely a symbolism of spirit. Spirit is realistic while culture and social life are symbolical. In the object there is never any reality, but only the symbol of reality. The subject alone always has reality. Therefore in objectification and in its product, the objective spirit, there can be no sacred reality, but only its symbolism. In the objective history of the world nothing transpires but a conventional symbolism; the idea of sacredness is peculiar to the existential world, to existential subjects. The real depths of spirit are apprehensible only existentially in the personal experience of destiny, in its suffering, nostalgia, love, creation, freedom and death. The primal aspect of religion is existential, spiritual and real. In the course of objectification it exchanges its real premises for symbolical ones. This particular symbolism should not be interpreted idealistically as the symbolism of man's psychic state, but realistically as the symbolism of the primal realities of being. Symbols can also be accepted as realities, but then it becomes more difficult to rediscover the true realities. The very idea of revelation is thus objectified. This tendency is particularly noticeable in most authoritarian ecclesiastical conceptions. In this sense revelation is represented as a penetration into man of an objective material reality or system of concepts to which real meaning is attached. This is an example of naïve realism which fails to take the subject's agency into account. But naïve realism is itself an illusion of consciousness engendered by the subject's objectifying agency. In this light spirit appears to be an abstraction, an emanation from without, from the object. The critique of revelation is concerned with purifying it from naïve objectification; it suggests that revelation should be interpreted as the agency of spirit on spirit, as the agency of the Divine Spirit on the human spirit, on human freedom, on human consciousness and conscience, all of which are themselves agents. Revelation is an event within the spiritual life wherein the voice of God alone is audible. In the secondary process of spiritual materialization, objectified revelation appears to be an external event derived from the object. But a faithful and loving communion with Christ is not the material thing it appears to be in the light of objectification: it is communion with the subject, the Thou; it is an existential communion. Communion with God is likewise communion with the subject. The agency of one subject on another is unlike that of constraining objectivity. Authority is such a constraining objectivity, but it does not imply the agency of one subject on another or of one spirit on another. Authority is the typical product of objectification, the typical product of a mass of human subjects, the typical symbolization of the subjects' spiritual state, of their servility, spiritual immaturity, self-abstraction. The part played by authority in the history of social life is tremendous. But in the sphere of authentic spiritual reality God is in no sense an authority; nor is revelation, for in that sphere there is no objectivity to condition the symbolical illusion of authority. In his uncertainty man seeks an authority on which he can rely; but such an authority is merely the product of his weakness, the projection of his subjectivity, of his failure to discover another, concretely-universal world. As it happens, authority does nothing to free man from his prison. The interpretation of anything in terms of external objectivity implies man's limitation and inability to transcend himself. Authority is the tyranny of the generic over the individual principle. In short, this objectification gives rise to the illusion that the universals govern personal existence.

Such are the forms of socialized religion. The spiritual life is involved in this process, which demonstrates man's failure to achieve the Kingdom of God. Even the Holy Spirit is objectified in the Church as a social institution. That is part of the social adaptation by which the human masses accustom themselves to the everyday world and the abstraction of their spirit. Spirituality persists only on the peaks. But the Church is not only a social institution primarily concerned with the affairs of the world, it has also an existential significance. Thus the two ruling principles of the Church are authority and freedom. Conscience—man's spiritual depths, his place of communion with God—is also freedom, a guarantee against abstraction, objectification or use for any organized collective purpose. Spirit is pure and independent of social utility, that symbol of objectified life. In the social and historical sphere the Church obeys the laws of the objectified world, the dictates of utility, and its message of truth therefore loses its force. Truth is essentially spiritual; it not only has no worldly utility, but may be prejudicial to organized life. Truth is an explosion in the world. The pure truth of the Christian revelation would mean the end of the objectified world. But historical Christianity has compromised by adapting this truth to the needs of society. Authentic Christianity founded on truth would bring about a personalistic revolution in the world. In the Gospel even the purity of spiritual revelation is troubled by the efficiency of the social environment, language and human limitations. Spirit can never be completely expressed in history, for it tends to symbolize rather than realize itself therein. The phenomenology of revelation should serve to confirm the truth that spirit or freedom exercises a primacy over all forms of objectified existence. Authentic holiness is peculiar to spirit rather than to nature, history or society, ecclesiastical or otherwise. Perfection is not the property of the finite, but of the infinite (ἄπειρον), of infinite creativeness. The objectification of spirit gives rise to collectives which claim to be a sort of objective spirit. But the existential spiritual community is in no sense objective spirit. The spiritual community, the *Sobornost*, may exist in every personality or subjective spirit, but it cannot be a sum. This spiritual community is the universal qualitative content of the subjective personal spirit, realizing itself only in the spiritual world. The collective spirit is secondary and objectified. The growth of spirit can divide as well as unite.

Objectification is the outcome of the relation of subjects to each other, and of the subject to the universal whole. Therefore the process may be considered from either a positive or a negative standpoint. Objectification is associated with the fallen, divided and fettered world. But in the process of being objectified spirit helps to establish ties in the fallen world, to apprehend the world in terms of the Fall and to organize it. In this sphere symbolization takes the place of realization. The act of human creation alone transcends fallen objectified time, but the materialization of creative achievements once more reintroduces time, limiting consciousness and arresting infinity. But spirit is distinct from both unconsciousness and limited consciousness. Spirit is super-consciousness. Objectified spirit is submission to the limitations of consciousness. Objectification is involved in a rationalized world, in a world of concepts. Hence the mystery of existence is lost sight of in this world. The final triumph of spirit would mean the annihilation of the non-authentic objective world, the achievement of the existential plane, the realization of authentic existence, the victory of reality over symbol. Authentic love is, indeed, such a realization. The problem is how to actualize spirit, how to take it out of its potential state without at the same time objectifying and abstracting it, or projecting existence into the fallen world.

That epitomizes the spiritual problem of creation. It implies that spirituality should be realized but not symbolized, realized existentially rather than objectively. Man is an incarnate spirit; and his vocation is creative incarnation. But incarnation is not identical with objectification. It permits of communion between the Ego and Thou. Such is incarnate love, real love, as opposed to symbolical love revealing itself only in attributes. Objectification usually becomes involved in symbols; and the objective world is indicative rather than real. In the sphere of knowledge objectification elaborates concepts and rationalizes actuality; disdaining the individual in human relationships, it works out forms of state, law and family incompatible with the inner existence and mystery of the personality; in the moral life, it establishes norms which are incapable of illuminating or effectively transforming human life; in the religious sphere, it propounds dogmas, canons and institutes which only obscure man's real relationship with God and with his neighbour. In a certain sense the whole visible objective edifice can be regarded merely as a symbolism of the spiritual world. The objectifying processes at work upon spirit inspire pessimistic reflections; but even the most pessimistic view of the historical objectification of spirit is unable to undermine our faith in man and his creative vocation. Historical objectification is the path of division which man must tread, the experience of destiny which he must face and in which he becomes alienated from himself, in order that he may later rediscover himself. In his culture, State, national and domestic life, in all these he has to experience the objectification of spirit. This is the tragedy of spirit as revealed in history.

II

Spirit is creative activity: every creative act is a spiritual act. But the creative act of the subjective spirit is an exteriorization of self in the world. In every creative act there is an element of

the primordial freedom inherent in the subjective spirit, an element free from external determination. The human creative act,
always of spiritual rather than natural origin, postulates the
material world, the plural human world; and emanating from
spirit, it introduces into the world something new and hitherto
non-existent. The creative act of spirit is both an ascent and a
descent. In its creative urge and flight spirit rises above the world
and dominates it, but the gravity of the world also pulls it down
and makes it conform in its products to the state of the world.
Thus spirit objectifies itself in its creative products, and in this way
establishes communication with the given state of the plural
world. Spirit is fire, its creativeness is flame. Objectification is the
death of the creative fire of spirit. Cultural objectification implies
a compromise with others, with the normal world, with social
environment. Spirit objectified in culture is socialized spirit, for
culture is a social phenomenon. This explains the importance of
tradition. The aristocratic principle in culture—a principle without which culture would not exist—is in no way opposed to its
socialized character. At the same time culture is symbolical, its
achievements are symbolical rather than real. The classical ideal
is the perfect objectification of spirit in culture, in science, in
philosophy, in art, in the ethical and social order. Classicism is
complete creative objectification, the imprisonment of spirit in a
finite and perfect form. The subjective becomes the objective, the
infinite becomes the finite, and in these dead forms the creative
fire is extinguished. The fiery infinite urge of spirit is made the
servant of social actuality. This subjugation of spirit is manifest
in the historical Church, in those who follow the letter of the
law, in Pharisees, in lifeless authoritarian systems, in the State, in
legalistic morality, in formalistic art, in the pseudo-classicism of
academies, in the legally established family and its suppression of
love, and in other institutions of a similar character. Spirit is incarnated both really and existentially in the human personality, in
its creatively intuitive attitude to life, in a fraternal communion

with other men. In objectifying itself in culture and in social life
spirit easily forgoes its freedom. The subjective spirit is no longer
itself as the so-called *objective spirit*. The premise of an objective
spirit, as for example in Hegel, leads to monism, and to the
tyranny of the general over the individual as in totalitarian systems.
There is no greater error than historical pantheism. History is not
the revelation of the objective spirit, for history is in fact discon-
tinuous. History is rather the tragedy of spirit. Thus, in the process
of historical objectification spirit is transformed into its opposite.
The creative subjective spirit is transmuted in its historical
forms. The Christian revelation is unrecognizable in historical
Christianity. There is little of St. Francis in Franciscanism.
Luther has been deformed in the history of Protestantism. There
is no trace of Leonardo da Vinci in the later development of
technical invention. The historical achievements of revolutions
belie their original spirit. Marx no longer stands for the same
principles in the light of subsequent Marxism. *Freedom, Equality
and Fraternity* have no reality in the societies professing this ideal.
The fiery creative spirit is unrecognizable in its products, in books,
theories, systems, artistic works, institutes. Historical and cultural
objectification is a great achievement of the active creative spirit,
but it is also a confession of a great failure. I do not mean that
spirit should never objectify itself. On the contrary, the world
and history should come to an end, the objectified world should
perish and should be supplanted by an existential world—a world
of authentic reality and freedom. The essential longing of the
creative fire of genius has always been that this determined and
objective world should be consumed and replaced by a free and
creative world. Historical objectification and culture have contributed only the symbols, signs and prefigurations of a real transfiguration.

It might be stated, as Marx does, that the greatest reality of all
is the struggle waged for technical supremacy by spirit against
nature in the economic sphere. But Marx himself put forward

the view that human nature was abstracted in the economic sphere. Man becomes a slave of the economic system he creates. He masters nature, but economic laws in turn dominate him. This same is true of technique, which is a great human achievement but which has become an anti-human instrument. Spirit is enslaved in the process of economic objectification. This is most clearly apparent in Capitalist economy. The power of money is a false product of objectification, an abstraction of human existence. Socialism is the revolt against this fiction: its goal is the subjectivization of human existence, but its economy threatens to betray its spiritual purpose. There is a tendency in the world to aim at absolute objectification, to arrive at a finally objectified and socialized spirit. Then spirit would be an abstraction and the mystery of existence would be no more. But spirit is freedom. The objectification of spirit is therefore a violation of spirit; abstraction transforms spirit itself into an instrument of violence. The State is one of the forms assumed by the objectified spirit; another is sovereignty, which claims to be of spiritual origin and which has been held sacred.

The objectification of spirit in the Church has led to false notions of sanctity. Thus, under the aegis of the greatest number, important masses of mankind were organized, and the attempt was made to organize and consolidate society and the State on the foundation of spiritual principles. The objectification of spirit in the life of societies and States is dictated by the utilitarian delusion that a society, State or civilization can be founded on truth, and that truth can serve a useful purpose in the sphere of human organization. This is a pragmatic interpretation of truth, a belief in the coincidence of truth and utility. But that is merely an illusion, an attempt at a compromise between spirit and the fallen world. Actually, the organized world is founded on socially useful falsehood rather than on truth. This admittedly serviceable falsehood rules the world. In this way the very truth of Christianity has been transformed into a socially useful fiction. Truth, pure truth, can be dangerous and destructive; it has no social utility and is of no practical help to men. Truth can be an upheaval, a judgment, an end of the world. Pure Christian truth, unde- formed and uncompromising, might prove to be destructive and anarchical. Truth is spiritually revolutionary just as spirit is revolutionary, but this must not be interpreted in any political sense. Moreover, objectification weakens or completely kills this *destructive* and *anarchical* element of truth—of spirit, that is, as the truth of being. Hence the coming of Christ was interpreted and adapted to the average needs of a billion men. The destinies of the world and of man are the tragic consequence of the radical dualism of truth and utility, of the subjective personal spirit and the objective general spirit, of existence and objectification. Truth is revealed only in the subjective spirit, it is existential. In the objective spirit truth is made use of and its existential quality is lost sight of. In the objective spirit truth is not realized, but sym- bolized and made rhetorical. The triumph of spirit in society would be a triumph of personalism, of personal communion, of the relation of one personality to another in a human and humane We, the recognition of the supreme value of every personality. This is the creation of a *subjective* rather than an *objective* society. But it would be a grave error to associate the personalistic and subjective character of a society with individualism. It is rather a personalistic and subjective sociality, the triumph of the existen- tial plane in which the personality is always transcending itself in community, rising above the objective plane. That would be a real revolution in human society—not merely a change of habit, of conventional symbolism, of a mode of objectifying or abs- tracting human nature. A society without objects, in which no man or thing will be treated as an object, such a society will, indeed, be the kindom of spirit and freedom; and in a sense it will be the coming of the Kingdom of God. This is not the objectifi- cation but the incarnation of spirit. Objectification and its accom- panying abstraction are the result of man's failure to seek the

Kingdom of God. But in this state of the world objectification has also a positive aspect. In that consists the whole difficulty of the problem. For objectification is preferable to a self-affirming and hermetic subjectivity. But the real spiritualization of man, society, the world, is diametrically opposed to the ways of objectification. For example, the existence of a *national* spirit is no proof of the existence of an *objective* spirit. When we speak of a *national* spirit we denote an authentically existing reality; this term is, of course, inexact, because we are referring to a nature and individuality rather than a spirit and personality. There exists, indeed, a national individuality in the sense of a natural psychic centre in which spirit is active, and which it is its task to spiritualize. But the notion of *national* spirit is usually interpreted in a symbolical rather than a realistic way, without any awareness of this symbolism.

As we have already established, the objectification of spirit gives rise to symbols rather than realities. The objectified world is in all its spheres a symbolical structure, although it claims to be a reality and is accepted as such. A person who is completely and finally involved in the objectified world and in objectified activity fails to grasp or to perceive the symbolical structure of which he is a part; and he regards himself as a realist. But symbolization and realization of spirit are two very different functions. The latter alone is an incarnation of spirit; objectification is no such thing. The extinction of the objectified spirit is in no sense a reincarnation. The objectification of spirit in the Church as a social institution is a symbolism, from which even the mystery and reality of cult are not free. Ritual and ceremonial are a form of conventional symbolism. The Christian commandments are thus symbolized rather than realized. Christian love and charity are expressed in conventional symbols rather than in realities. The relation of the various grades in the ecclesiastical hierarchy to each other, and their relation to laymen, is regulated according to such a conventional symbolism. The ecclesiastical parish is not so much

E

a Christian community as a symbolism of it. In dogmas and in
the mysteries symbolism triumphs over realism. This is the
Christian nominalism of which Rozanov spoke. It explains, too,
the excessive part played by rhetoric in Christian ritual. Symbolism also supplants realism in married and family life. In most
cases marriage is a symbolical rather than a real sacrament founded
on love. Family relationships likewise tend to be conventional
and ritualistic, leaving comparatively little room for the impetus
of realities. The life of the State is, of course, entirely symbolical.
Symbols and signs are the prerogative of authority; and the cere-
mony with which it surrounds itself has nothing in common with
reality. Formalities, decorations, dicipline are all the paraphernalia
of armies and warfare. Titles such as Tsar, general, Pope, metro-
politan, bishop are all symbols. All hierarchical grades are symbols.
In contradistinction to them we have such realities as Saint,
prophet, creative genius, social reformer. Thus the hierarchy of
human qualities is real. The whole of man's moral and ethical
life is a symbolical structure rather than a real transfiguration of
human beings. Legalistic morality exacts from men the perform-
ance of conventional acts having no necessary, real connection
with their inner life and spirituality. The fulfilment of obligations
is also a symbolical act. The current symbolism of communication between men hardly corresponds to any reality. So-called
good deeds, charity itself, can be symbolical. Hypocrisy is an extreme form of symbolism and unreality. The objectified world
pays no heed to the living concrete personality but is concerned
with objects, the reality of which is inapprehensible. Men's relation to objects is always symbolical. The same is true of knowledge, scientific or philosophical; formal academism propounds
methods of dealing with the object but fails to apprehend reality,
for which living intuition is necessary. Mathematics, the most
completely objectified branch of knowledge, has evolved a symbolism which is easily grasped by a spiritually disintegrated world.
Objective scientific methods are symbolical. Perfect knowledge

is achieved independently of the primal realities, just as perfect justice is administered independently of real relationships between men. Men live in the objectified world as if it were a real world, whereas it is actually a world of attributes and symbols; and an objective interpretation of it, although it helps to establish communications of general validity, is still a symbolical one. It seems paradoxical that the spiritual life, the real life, should also be symbolized. That is apparent in the various forms of asceticism which symbolize rather than realize the spiritual life. Historic Christianity was on the whole symbolical rather than realistic. The whole hierarchical spiritual structure is symbolical and opposed to human reality, replacing the real man by a symbolical gradation. Symbolization is, in fact, a socially organizing force. It is operative in all revolutions—as, for example, in the symbolical idea of the *proletariat* as distinct from the reality of the worker. The problem of sanctification is intimately connected with symbolization.

The historical objectification of spirit gives rise to sanctification, to the illumination of certain elements of natural and human life. Certain consecrated parts objectifying spirituality stand out from the sinful body of the world. They might be forms of spiritual or temporal authority, or the objects of a cult. Man has a deep-seated need of the sacred not only in heaven but also on earth; he has need of spirit in a tangible and visible form. A sacred character has been attributed to most diverse manifestations: the State, the nation, the family, property, society, culture, civilization. This implies, of course, that spirit is objectified and translated into these forms. Sanctification is invariably symbolization. In this world sanctity is not a sacred reality, but the symbol of that sacred reality. Sanctity is symbolized in anointed hierarchs, in material objects sprinkled with holy water. Thus sanctity is not human, it is the revelation of human spirituality. In it spirit is represented by attributes and symbols. There is a gulf between accepting the sanctity of an anointed sacred hierarchy and of objects on the one

hand, and that of the human subject himself, his holiness, creativeness, freedom, love, fraternity, knowledge, beauty of soul, on
the other. The former is symbolical, the latter is realistic. In the
former spirit objectifies itself, in the latter spirit is revealed in
existence itself. Spirit is historically incarnated in hierarchical
authority, in historical bodies, in authority, whereas spirit is really
incarnated in truth, in man's creative emancipation from slavery.
The symbolical incarnation of spirit is merely a way determined
by the fallen world, while the real incarnation of spirit is the goal,
the supreme achievement. It is above all necessary to grasp this
process of symbolization, to expose it and also to distinguish it
from realization. It would, however, be an error to regard symbolization as a purely negative process.

The symbolical interpretation of the world, according to which
everything perceptible is a symbol of the imperceptible, everything material a symbol of the spiritual, is a sign of greater spirituality in relation to the world and of greater freedom from the
world. Such was, for example, the medieval symbolism of Hugh
and Richard. The consciousness that anything in this world is
merely the symbol of another world has the effect of liberating
man from a slavish dependence on this world. It is to perceive
the purpose underlying an otherwise meaningless world. It is not
a form of objectification, but on the contrary a return of the objective world to the sphere of inner existence. It is quite a different
thing from attributing a symbolical sanctity to the objects of this
world, from making man a slave of the object and thus prevent-
ing his realization of reality. The symbolism of saintliness is an
obstacle to real saintliness. The symbolical sanctity of rank clashes
with the real sanctity of man. That is a fundamental distinction
in the doctrine of spirit. Spirit and the spiritual life are not symbolical, but realistic. The objectification of spirit in the natural
and historical world is symbolical. The incarnation of spirit cannot in itself signify the sanctification of authority and of the hierarchy, the preservation of historical bodies on the ground of their

sanctity. In reality incarnation implies the descent of the Divine Spirit and its union with real human and world destiny. Spirit is never incarnate in the instincts of man's domination over his fellow-men. Nor can spirit be really incarnate in discursive scientific thought, in formal legalistic morality and law, in any objective form. But spirit does incarnate itself in the real ascent of the subject, of the personality towards God, and in the real descent of Divine love and charity towards the subject, in the intuitive communion of the knowing with the known, in the real creation of the hitherto non-existent, in original judgment. Creativeness is not objectification, but trans-subjectification. The objective should be replaced by the trans-subjective.

German philosophers have admitted that spirit was apprehended not in objective nature, but in history and culture. But it must be said that, although the historical and cultural world is nearer to the existential subject than the natural world of physico-mathematical science, this world is nevertheless an objectified world, abstracted from the existential subject. On the other hand, *nature* has also an existential purpose. Thus the Romatics turned to 'nature', an embodiment for them of freedom, truth, creative power and infinity, as an escape from convention, falsehood, determinism and civilization with its tyrannical norms and laws. This led to a confusion of terms. For freedom, truth and infinity are the qualities of spirit and spirituality, whereas determinism, legalism and finality are the qualities of nature. In this context, nature is objectification, the world of objects and things, the mechanical sphere determined from without, rather than the animal and vegetable world. Spiritual realism, the real ascent and descent, is opposed to this sphere of objectified spirit with its accompanying symbolism and sanctity. *Kenosis*, the Divine incarnation, the descent of God into the human world, is a form of spiritual realism to which processes in the human world should correspond. But symbolical sanctity has taken the place of the realization of the Gospel commandments. And that was the historical tragedy of Christianity. The causes of this are obvious: Christian spirituality became involved in the objectified fallen world, with the result that it was adapted to the state of that world. In this case the objectification of spirit implied its exteriorization rather than its incarnation or a real descent of Divine love into the world. The objectification of spirit was not only a fact determined by the condition of the world, but it was also established as a sacred principle. Spirit was made one with nature in the sense of objectivity and determination.

The development of technique and its increasing power over man is of tremendous importance in the destinies of the spiritual life. Technique appears as a despiritualizing force in human life. If incarnation is organic, then technique is not only a despiritualizing but also a disincarnating force. The machine divorces spirit from the organic body. The triumph of technique seriously affects all the historical *organic* bodies. It proclaims the end of the tellurgic period of history, a transition from the *organism* to *organization*. Machinery and technique introduce not only a new period of human history, but also a new cosmic period. Side by side with organic and non-organic bodies there appear organized bodies such as have never before existed. But although technique dehumanizes man, it is a product of the human spirit. Human creativity has brought into being hitherto non-existent cosmic forces. The technical organization of human life implies an extreme form of objectification. It transforms the human body into an instrument, into a technical function. But the relation between spirit and technique is more complex than is commonly supposed, for technique can also be a spiritualizing force. For the Romantics spirit and organism were intimately blended. That is one way of interpreting incarnated spirit. Spirit is incarnated in the organism—not only in the human body but also in the organic historical bodies, in national life, tradition and so forth. That is the source of the Romantic reaction against technique which disrupts the organism. Technique plunges man into an atmosphere of cold metal, it eliminates human warmth. But if spirit were entirely dependent on material conditions, whether positive or negative, on external historical and organic forms, then that would denote a terrible limitation of the reality of spirit. No change in human conditions can do away with the reality of spirit. Such changes are merely the sign that spirituality is faced with a crisis. There is a crucifixion of man preceding the birth of a new life, before the dawn of a new spirituality. Technique has turned against man, for he was unable to master it. Nevertheless technique is a manifestation of the human spirit in the world. It testifies to man's creative vocation in the cosmic life. The machine has a fatal effect on man's emotional life. It subordinates man to the increasing tempo of time, for which each instant is but the means of attaining the next. It makes contemplation increasingly difficult. Technique actualizes human life and makes ever greater demands on human activity. But the technical domination of human life implies man's passivity, his helplessness in face of the world and its processes. That is one aspect of technique. But there is another. In the presence of technique man's salvation requires extraordinary spiritual concentration and activity, extraordinary powers of resistance. It is a great trial of man's spiritual strength. When plunged in organic life and protected by its slow rhythm, spirituality was diffused and insufficiently concentrated. Thus man will be called upon to enter a period of a more heroic and actualized spirituality. Spirit is now situated between the organic and the technical life, but it must become freer, more independent of both the organic and the technical conditions of its realizations. Technique can become the instrument of spirit, of spiritual realization. This is a critical moment in the history of the objectified spirit. In the process of objectification spirit becomes subordinated to objects. Technique is the expression of the power of objects over spirit. Spirit is in danger of finally becoming objectified. But according to the law of polarity governing human existence spirit is mastering the objectivity of technique, and can transform it into an instrument of spiritualization, an instrument for humanizing cosmic and social life. As is always the case, the transition period is terrifying and torturing; it is an experience of death. The passage from organic incarnation, in which man was at the mercy of cosmic forces, to organized and technical incarnation, in which man becomes the master of the cosmos, is an inner moment in the history of spirit. In this connection, when considering the different types of spirituality, it is important to investigate the relation between technique and asceticism.

CHAPTER IV.

THE AIM OF ASCETICISM

I

The Christian consciousness, as well as religious consciousness in general, admit certain obstacles and difficulties which must be resolved before the spiritual life is attainable. At different times and in different ways man has been conscious of sin, of an ancient burden of guilt, of his participation in a fallen world. This was an expression of his deep feeling for life; and if modern man has lost the sense of sin and of the Fall, it is a sign that he has also lost his spirituality and is leading a superficial existence at the mercy of the world. Modern man is profoundly unhappy and that explains, perhaps, his obsession with the absurd idea that happiness can be organized. He is immeasurably inferior to the wise men of antiquity—Confucius, Buddha, the Stoics. Even Epicureanism, which was on the whole a shallow and frivolous philosophy, was a more interesting manifestation than modern materialism. Passions and desires not only debase human nature, but also deform the spiritual life itself. Man's relation to God, his love of his neighbour, his apprehension of truth and his realization of justice can all be distorted by passion. The development of the spiritual life implies purification, a renouncement of worldly power with its concomitants of desire and lust. The austerity of Christian asceticism was a reaction against the pagan world, an expression of the necessity to dominate elemental barbarity. That was the problem of physical asceticism which concentrated on the body. The term *asceticism* lends itself to various interpretations and uses. In the first place, it can be interpreted in a broad, comprehensive and formal manner. Asceticism has no immediate solutions to offer for the problems of evil and sin. In the literal

69

sense of the word, asceticism means exercise and may be practised
in various spheres and for different ends. It is a concentration of
man's inner forces and a mastery of self. Man has need of discipline, of renouncement and concentration, in order to achieve
complete mastery over himself and to attain effectively his goal
whatever it may be, spiritual or athletic. Man should not be a
slave either of himself, his baser nature or his environment. In
this sense asceticism implies man's liberation.

A limitation of human necessities is postulated not only by
Christianity or man's spiritual renascence, but by man's conscious
attitude to life or any goal. Epicurus himself insisted upon it.
There is an athletic as well as a spiritual asceticism. The former is
probably the only form of asceticism acceptable to modern man.
Sport entails risks necessitating serious physical as well as spiritual
training. The danger of death is sometimes present and the sports-
man must be prepared to face that risk. Technical discoveries and
inventions, stratosphere ascents or submarine exploration, for
example, demand some degree of asceticism and sometimes
heroic asceticism. There is also a type of revolutionary asceticism.
All revolutionary movements imply an ascetic attitude before
victory is achieved. Indeed, a revolutionary victory would be
impossible without a foundation of asceticism. Rachmetov, the
hero of Chernishevsky's utopian novel, *What Shall We Do?*,
sleeps on a bed of nails to train himself to suffering and even
torture. In this Nechayev's *Revolutionary Catechism* is of particular
interest. Nechayev was a blend of fanatic and zealot; he was a
heroic ascetic who justified the use of immoral and inhuman
means. His *Revolutionary Catechism* gives the impression of an
ascetic tract, its precepts requiring from the revolutionary a
complete renouncement of the world. The revolutionary must
have no love to spare for the world or anything in it. Thus there
is an affinity of principle with the ascetic, spiritual and mystical
life. There is the same necessity of renouncing the plural world,
of exclusive preoccupation with the One, of love and sacrifice

for the One. The One in Nechayev's case is the revolution. The old plural world is judged to be wholly evil and sinful. The revolutionary is himself a doomed man. He has sacrificed his private interests, affairs, feelings, attachments, personality and even his name. His whole being is dominated by one supreme interest, one idea, one passion,—the revolution. The revolutionary repudiates civil life, the civilized world, civilized morality. A man is no revolutionary who values anything in this world. Thus revolutionary asceticism appears to be a distorted aspect of religious asceticism. The goal may be quite different but the psychological resemblance is very strong. This is proof that asceticism may be interpreted formalistically, quite independently of its original religious and metaphysical postulates. A strictly formal comparison can be drawn between Nechayev and St. Isaac the Syrian or St. Ignatius Loyola, but their goals were, of course, very different. The aim of all asceticism is to strengthen the will power.

But asceticism may also be interpreted more appropriately as a metaphysical and religious principle. Ascetic metaphysics postulates the problem of evil and its resolution. There are two principal forms of ascetic metaphysics. The first interprets both the world and life as evil. This is the position of Hindu metaphysics, in so far as it regards the world as illusion and evil. Buddhism is within limits an expression of ascetic metaphysics. Greek ascetic metaphysics, on the other hand, assumes a different form. In the first place, ascetic metaphysics is peculiar to Orphism. Matter, the *meon*, is the source of evil. Thus later Greek pessimism in its nostalgic quest for oblivion came to regard the whole material world as evil. Neo-Platonism is a form of ascetic metaphysics preaching the renouncement of the material world. In Plotinus the material world is evil because it is mixed with *meonic* matter. Through asceticism man must renounce the plural world and find deliverance in the One. Greek thought invariably considered matter as the source of evil, although it interpreted matter

in a different way from Descartes and the thinkers of the nineteenth and twentieth centuries. Persian dualism, on the other
hand, admits a dual divinity, a good and an evil god. Evil is
substantial; there is an evil being. Thus Manicheism is an extreme
form of this dualism. Gnosticism, with its abhorrence of matter,
is also largely dualistic. In this type of metaphysics the material
principle cannot be transfigured and illuminated, it can only be
severed from the spiritual principle; for the lowest cannot be
raised to the level of the highest. This type of asceticism implies
division, the divorce of the spiritual from the material principle.
The spiritual is restored to its proper sphere while the material
sinks back into its *meonic* state. Here the problem of evil is not
associated with that of freedom. As a result, nothing is essentially
changed; only the mixture is brought to an end. Evil matter
cannot be dominated, but only dissociated from oneself. Hence
asceticism is a renouncement of the plural mixed world. Spirit
can never be spiritualized matter, because matter would debase
it; escape from it is therefore the only solution. Hence man's
attainment of the ideal spiritual world implies his separation from
the material world. The agency of spirit in the world is not that
of transfiguring grace. This type of ascetic metaphysics precludes
man's deification. Man is a mixed product of spirit and matter.
Asceticism involves his disincarnation and dehumanization. As
a result, man fails to preserve his specific and original character.
Extreme monism is the pole of extreme dualism. And this is
eternally true. Ascetic metaphysics turns its back on love and
charity, on the mystery of the personality and freedom. Schopenhauer at least knows compassion, although he typifies an extreme
form of Buddhistic ascetic metaphysics for which being is evil.
There is neither love nor compassion, but only austerity in Neo-
Platonic asceticism and in Gnosticism with its sharp antithesis
between pneumatic and psychic or physical elements. It seems
paradoxical that the Gnostic struggle against matter could assume
contrary forms: an ascetic renouncement of the flesh or a morti-

fication of the flesh through debauch. This attitude has, of course, nothing in common with Plotinus, who held no brief for the Gnostics.

Christian asceticism is different, because it is based on a different kind of metaphysics. It differs completely in its approach to the metaphysical and religious problems of evil. Christian metaphysics in its purer forms does not regard the world as being essentially evil, but as fallen and sinful. The source of evil lies in freedom and in the will rather than in matter or any kind of *nature*. Evil is not the plural world or any kind of material substance, but those voluntarily determined relations which assume solid and inert material forms. Neither Neo-Platonism, Gnosticism nor Manicheism grasped the problem of freedom. This failure explains why their asceticism did not become an illumination of the lowest, and the transfiguration of the lowest into the highest. It implied, instead, the renouncement or the annihilation of the lowest. Christianity, on the other hand, does not repudiate man and the world, as the monistic metaphysics of identity is apt to do. Christianity is divinely human. Actually, it does not encourage us to love the *world* and its manifestations; but in this context the *world* is not a Divine creation nor the various forms of cosmic and human life, but a sinful and fallen state of the world. When the Fathers of the Church spoke of the *world*, they intended the sinful passions. Our life is confined to a false, non-authentic world; its ties should not be binding for us and we should aspire after a different world.

In philosophical and gnosiological terms I call this fallen world the *objectified* world. It is the sphere of determinism and material inertia. It is the world of everyday sociality. But a different orientation of the will, a spiritual urge, an impulse of freedom, can transform this state of the world. From the existential standpoint the plural world, human plurality, are not an evil that must be eradicated or annihilated, but rather one that must be illuminated and transfigured. There is a greater element of truth in pluralism than in monism. In this light spiritualization can be a triumph over the objectified material world without at the same time being a disincarnation. The *flesh* is as much part of the existential plane as of the objectified one. Christian asceticism, which is itself in need of being purified from extraneous elements, helps to liberate the body from the power of the lower elements by acting spiritually upon it. In this sense, asceticism is a concentration of strength in the body as an instrument of spirit rather than as a mortification or neglect of the body. But Christian asceticism was penetrated by Neo-Platonic, Stoic and Manicheistic elements and, as a result, there was a tendency for asceticism to practice indifference to and abhorrence of the creature. It was assumed that the repudiation, the renouncement of the plural world—of the whole created world, of human plurality—was an inevitable condition of loving communion with the One. But actually, this was a violation of the dual Gospel commandment of *love God* and *love thy neighbour*. Thus there was a transformation and degeneration of asceticism: it became a goal in itself rather than a means to an end. The notion of sin came to hold a paramount place in ascetic mediation. The consequences of this were fatal. Monastic asceticism frequently encouraged not only indifference but also ill-will towards the creature and fellow-men. The creature was represented as a temptation, as a sinful being. Thus asceticism has both a positive and a negative aspect. Sinful passions could be combated by the awakening of man's positive, creative and spiritual forces, by directing his will to higher ends. Negative and destructive passions could be transformed, as the material of the vital process, into positive and beneficent ones, into creative passions serving spirit. This was the intention of the Fathers of the Church. Positive asceticism was a struggle waged against sin and sinful servitude by the help of creative spirit and creative love. Negative asceticism, on the other hand, aimed at crushing and annihilating the sinful passions; and this evinces its failure to direct these passions towards positive creation or to inspire love for positive creative values. Inhibition is the result of suppressed passions; and its consequences have been studied by Freud and the psychoanalysts. Human nature is deformed, and the value of man's latent positive spiritual forces is distrusted. Sin becomes man's only preoccupation: he detects sin everywhere, in himself and in others; he becomes a negative being hostile to life. But experience teaches us that sin is more effectively overcome in a positive than in a negative way—through the awakening of love, knowledge, creation, through an aspiration towards the beautiful, noble and the sublime.

The teaching of the Gospel is not ascetic in the sense in which some of the later Christian writings were ascetic. It will suffice to compare the Gospel with *The Love of Virtue* or *The Imitation of Christ*, to perceive the difference in style consequent upon a distinction in spiritual essence. The Gospel is the Word of God, ascetic writings are the works of men. In the Gospel there is, indeed, an element of formal asceticism, but there is no ascetic metaphysics such as is found, for example, in Neo-Platonism. The Gospel is a Messianic book—a revolutionary-Messianic book if you like—rather than a strictly ascetic one. In the Bible, in Judaism, there was no asceticism as in Hindu philosophy, Orphism, Neo-Pythagorism, Neo-Platonism. In the Hellenistic world asceticism made its appearance considerably later. The path of prophetic inspiration was not that of asceticism. Far from repudiating or renouncing the world, the nations and humanity, prophecy confronts and serves them. Prophecy is not a school or way of spiritual development by successive stages. The prophet has other means at his disposal for conquering the world. Messianism is very different from asceticism. The Gospel is permeated with a human Judaic atmosphere, and it has little in common with the aims and methods of the Hindu and Greek ascetic or mystical schools. In His human image Jesus Christ does not in the least remind us of an ascetic. If He had not had the experience of temptation, He would not have been human, He would not

also have been a man. This experience is the lot of every man who
embarks upon a saintly or heroic path. But Jesus Christ did not
disdain the plural world, the human world in all its misery; He
did not renounce the sinful world, but, on the contrary, went out
to meet it and mingle with it. He spent His life among men,
among sufferers, among sinners; He also appeared at feasts. The
Pharisees reproached Him for this, for not observing the rules of
purity, for frequenting the impure. The Gospel is the glad tidings
of the coming of the Kingdom of God rather than an ascetic
manual for the salvation of the soul. The Gospel is not in itself
the foundation of any ascetic school; for asceticism is a school and
method, a patient path of perfection and development. The
Gospel speaks of a new birth, of a blissful spiritual rebirth. It is
in every sense a spiritual impulse towards the world, with catastrophic, rather evolutionary implications. The thief's brief appeal
to Christ is answered, and he inherits the Kingdom of Heaven.
Sufferers and sinners lead the way to the Kingdom of Heaven.
The Gospel does not preach the individual salvation of the soul
through schooling or discipline. It is Messianic, it announces the
Kingdom of God. That is the essential difference. The Gospel
renouncement of the world is a Messianic and eschatological one.
Asceticism is individualistic; but the Gospel is social in the
religious sense of the word, in the sense in which *social* and *prophetic* are synonymous. In the light of this, man can fast, live in
poverty, sacrifice all earthly goods; but this will not be merely
an ascetic exercise for the sake of individual salvation. Sacrifice is
not necessarily asceticism, it can serve a different purpose. The
Gospel requires a sacrifice of love rather than ascetic discipline.
The Apostolic Church and early Christianity were free from
asceticism. The Christian martyrs were not ascetics. Asceticism
was a later growth. Its principle should not be defined in terms
of continence, limitation of necessities, renouncement of earthly
goods, or sacrifice of self for the sake of God or of one's neighbour, but in terms of its attitude to the world and man, the plural

and the One. The non-ascetic may in principle lead a more *ascetic* life than the professed ascetic—or, in other words, he may assume the burden of the plural created world and share its destiny. The ascetic principle is the antithesis of love. The Gospel does not recommend effusive prayer or preach salvation through solitary prayer; nor will Christ inquire into these matters on the Day of Judgment.

In the course of Christian history asceticism has undergone important transformations and has submitted to non-Christian influences. Monastic asceticism came into being after the mass conversion of the pagan world, after the Roman empire had adopted Christianity; it was, in fact, an attempt to arrest the spiritual corruption of Christianity. Previously, the Christians had been a spiritual *élite* at war with the pagan world, the pagan State. Their persecution had only helped to concentrate and intensify their spirituality. After Constantine the Great the Christians found themselves in a privileged position, with no external enemy to. persecute them. But then an internal enemy appeared against whom a war had to be waged. Christianity was assailed by growing prosperity and vulgarization, and it became necessary to form a sort of religious aristocracy to deal with the menace. Monasticism and monastic asceticism became the expression of this necessity, the focus of a higher and more intense spirituality. Monastic asceticism followed the path of greatest resistance, of heroic struggle against nature and the sinful passions. There are tremendous achievements to its credit. Asceticism had its period of growth and flowering. There were the anchorets, the Syrian and Egyptian asceticisms. The desert had its mirages and illusions, its demoniac visions. Syrian asceticism became interpenetrated by certain elements of Manichean dualism. It was not exclusively Gospel in character. But its original greatness is undeniable. It was one of the most remarkable phenomena in the history of the human spirit. Asceticism had not yet been modified by rules; it still represented an heroic urge to battle with and conquer a

F

world sunk in evil. A moderate asceticism like that of St. John
Cassianus aimed at purity of heart. By the flesh he designated not
the physical creature, but the corporeal will and evil desires. The
necessary degree of abstinence was to be judged by each individual
conscience. Pride was admitted as a universal passion. Salvation
was a matter of grace and freedom. Man was free and he freely
accepted the agency of grace. Such was the teaching of St.
Cassianus, who stood midway between the Eastern and the
Western modes of thought. In Eastern asceticism temperance
holds an important place in the struggle against the passions.
Temperance is purity of heart. The monk is he who renounces
passionate intentions. Holy Isaeus of Jerusalem preached that the
Kingdom of Heaven was not a reward for actions performed, but
a gift of grace. Thus the utilitarian principle had not yet penetrated into asceticism. Holy Nigel of Sinai taught that the means
used for controlling passions should not themselves be turned
into passions. Immaterial things should be treated immaterially.
The *world* was the passions engendered by the fumes of the mind.

But Syrian desert asceticism began to preach indifference to
the world. St. Gregory of Sinai regards it as the highest achievement. The *Love of Virtue* is permeated with this notion. The
motive of compassion will make itself heard more insistently in
Western Catholic mysticism. The ascetic authors of *The Love of
Virtue* hold that the monk is he who severing all his human ties
is yet one with all men. But this union is dispassionate and admits
of no attachment to any creature. The apparent consequences of
this doctrine are: *He that loveth the world suffereth greatly, but he
that despiseth the world hath always joy.* This doctrine of indifference
to the creature is pushed to its extreme where women are concerned. Ascetic writings are full of panic and fear inspired by the
idea of woman. This is true of the most profound of these writers,
St. Isaac the Syrian. According to him the virtue of renunciation
lies in the banishment of all worldly preoccupations from the
mind. When the vestiges of the created world are exorcised, then

the mind becomes filled with the Divine. Be friends with all men, but be with yourself in the mind. This uniform type of friendship lacks any personal element, any warmth. It is an example of a dispassionate attitude towards the creature. St. Maxim the Confessor, who is an exponent of practical asceticism and theoretical mysticism, says: *Happy is the man who can love everyone with the same degree of love.* He maintains that love is born of impartiality. He fails to achieve perfect love who is influenced by men's character, loving one, detesting another. This is a plea for perfect impartiality, for withholding love from the individual creature, for uniform love without soul or spirit. It betrays the influence of the Neo-Platonic renunciation of plurality and of Stoic apathy. But practical asceticism gets the better of philosophical mysticism.

St. John, the greatest authority on asceticism, says: *The sensual man is compassionate and merciful, but the seeker after truth is not such.* This is a remarkable passage. It would appear from it that the seeker after purity is neither compassionate nor merciful. The more humane are inclined to sensuality. This helps finally to establish the antithesis between the ascetic principle and that of love, compassion and mercy. In another passage St. John says: *To escape from sorrow man must hate the world; the love of God extinguishes the love of one's kindred and of all creatures.* Thus asceticism, ascetic purity imply the extinction of the psychic human element, the elimination of man's human content. Asceticism is within its limits anti-human. Ascetics are so preoccupied with themselves, with their purity and salvation, that they come to hate humanity and have no compassion to waste on it. The spiritual love after which they strive, and which almost no one ever achieves, will have no soul or human content. Love is born of fear. But it is not love or compassion which predominates, but renunciation of the will and obedience. St. John says that humility is the only thing demons cannot imitate. It would thus appear that they can love their neighbour, be charitable and compassionate. Ascetic metaphysics is in its principles hostile to man, it is opposed to God's love of man. Sadistic and masochistic instincts in idealized forms have played an important part in the spiritual life and have often determined the character of asceticism. There was a tendency to transform the struggle against sin into a struggle against humanity. It was against this that humanism very justifiably rebelled. Monastic asceticism not only transmuted the gospel of love into one of obedience, but it also perverted the very idea of obedience. The latter became a human affair; man, not God, was obeyed and served. Even St. Simon, the New Theologian, the greatest mystic of the Orthodox East, says: *Ask not a drop of water even to quench thy thirst unless thy spiritual father be moved of himself and bid thee do so.*

Thus the suppression of the human will would appear to be the greatest achievement of mysticism. Everything is subordinated to the war waged against sin. But extreme obedience and repentance vitiate the human conscience and human dignity. Asceticism may only harden the heart and instil fear of the impulses of the human soul. Constant attempts are made to intimidate men by pointing to the dangers of pride, and thus false meekness and obedience are encouraged. But meekness and obedience in their turn may easily lead to unconscious pride, the pride of the meek, as well as to ill-will and even malice. This, then, is the dialectic of the spiritual life. When all perceptible things are so much dust and smoke, then every man, every fellow-being, every creature may also appear to be worthless, mere dust and smoke. The attempt to eradicate every passion for worldly things may be a sign of indifference, coldness, ill-will and cruelty towards the created world, towards all living creatures. But it is also necessary to cultivate fear within oneself, the fear of God, for spiritual fearlessness only corrupts the soul. Indeed, in so far as asceticism is the expression of a Christian attitude hostile to life and to the world, of a constant consciousness of human sin and impotence, it is an impediment and a temptation in the spiritual life, a betrayal of spirit, a sadistic and masochistic impulse. In the light of such a conception no human creative effort is possible. Clement of Alexandria, who blended classical moderation with Stoic and Neo-Platonic elements, advocated *apathy*, which in its more extreme ascetical forms was also hostile to the world and man. A dispassionate state of the soul is an obedient one. The anchorets practised physical ascetic exercises reminiscent of the Hindu system. But these physical exercises were accompanied by a contempt for the body, a refusal to wash or care for it. Of the three vows of poverty, chastity and obedience, the last was the most respected in monastic asceticism. Poverty and chastity can be fully realized outside the monastic system. There was a tendency, likewise, to make the consciousness of sin an excuse for denigrating human dignity and humiliating man. Meekness was defined as consciousness of human worthlessness and nothingness rather than as a victory achieved at the expense of egocentricity and its phantasms.

II

The Imitation of Christ still holds its place as the classic of Christian asceticism and spiritual life. This book stands above any confessional differences. It is a splendid work: grave and sorrowful in tone, sensitive to the evil of this life, to man's bitter destiny. It expresses an eternal truth. It preaches repentance, but admits that repentance is worthless without grace and love. It calls upon man to examine the depths of his conscience. It proclaims that the loving man has wings, he lives in joy and freedom; that the man who does not value himself too high is free and safe; that communion with God is man's victory over himself. But in the *Imitation of Christ*, as in other ascetic writings, there is no love for perceptible things, for the plural created world. A thirst for knowledge is considered sinful. Man's greatest danger is above all impure love for the creature. All that is not God is worthless and must be treated accordingly. Man turns to God when no creature can console him. Life must appear to be endless death. Man must withdraw from his fellow-beings and retire into himself. It is better to suffer torments in this world than in the next. Man must seek peace in God. God says: You have need of Me, but I have no need of you. So far all this is typical of metaphysical asceticism in general. But a new and tremendously important attitude was introduced into the history of asceticism by St. Ignatius Loyola and the Society of Jesus. This particular asceticism was active and militant, concerned with the will rather than the body. It suppressed the individual will and made of man a living corpse, an embodiment of iron will directed to the conquest of the world for the glory of God. Spiritual exercise is action. The creature is a means of glorifying God, a means at the disposal of the army glorifying God. St. Ignatius Loyola insists on indifference towards all created things, all creatures. Everything is but an instrument in the hands of God. The creature must avenge the wrong done to God. Man does not sin, because he fears above all Hell. Mediation is more necessary between man and Hell than between man and the Kingdom of Heaven. The sadistic element is very strongly pronounced in Jesuit asceticism. There is nothing disinterested in this system; it is pedantic, mortifying and domineering. In contrast to the spirituality of the Orthodox East, Jesuit spirituality is founded on the principle of imagination. The elect of God might even be a king. St. Ignatius Loyola professes love for God but not for men. His God is vengeful. His love of one's neighbour is not the love of man. It appears ultimately that man must love himself more than God. Saintliness is absolute obedience. The Jesuit spirituality implies a far greater degree of human activity, and in this sense it is an expression of modern history. But that activity in no wise affirms human dignity. St. Ignatius Loyola advocated meditation, and in this respect his spiritual exercises are sometimes reminiscent of occultism. His is an essentially militant spirituality bent on conquering the world. Jesuitism defended the freedom of the will, particularly the doctrine of Molina. The

Molinists were engaged in a controversy with the Thomists. They represented an attempt to discard medieval spirituality. Their defence of the freedom of the will is utilitarian in character. Asceticism is interpreted legalistically. Asceticism appears to be a reward, and the doctrine of good deeds is associated with it. This interpretation of asceticism as a reward is common to official Catholic theology. But Catholic spirituality also propounded the remarkable and profound doctrine of man's participation in the matter of expiation, of salvation by means of compensating acts. This is associated with the intense experience of Calvary and of suffering in Christian mysticism, with the importance attached by Catholic saints and mystics to the care of the sick, with the tortures inflicted on themselves by those concerned not only with their own salvation but with that of others. This notion is alien to Eastern asceticism and mysticism. St. Catherine of Siena, for example, attaches great importance to her ability to overcome her repulsion for the smells associated with sickness and sick people. St. Ludvina spent her whole life in the midst of terrible maladies, but she believed in their redeeming quality. But the introduction of the utilitarian element into the conception of asceticism had as its consequence that the lofty impulse to participate in redemption, to be instrumental in the salvation of others, was abused and converted into a trade in indulgences, thus provoking Luther's stormy protest. There was formed a sort of capital of heavenly pardons controlled by the Pope. Such were the consequences of rationalizing a mystery.

In the Russian spiritual-ascetic literature of the nineteenth century Bishop Feofan the Hermit was the greatest authority. His book, *The Road to Salvation*, had the reputation of being the principal Russian work dealing with the spiritual life. This book is primarily ascetic, mysticism being subordinated to asceticism. Feofan the Hermit writes in the tradition of *The Love of Virtue*. We may discover in him, of course, certain eternal truths of asceticism as a method and a means. He establishes three stages in the spiritual life, arranged somewhat differently than was usual in the mystical tradition dating from the pseudo-Dionysius. These three stages are: communion with God, purification, illumination. But his system also reflects all the negative aspects of asceticism. There is a great deal of truth in him when he asserts that man's highest spiritual aspirations are the remnants of the Divine image in him, when he affirms the spiritual significance of suffering, or when he proposes to purify his mind of anxieties. But he is hostile to research or worldly philosophizing. He regards science as superfluous or accidental. He is afraid of youth and warns against its dangers. In short, he is hostile to the awakening of man's creative forces. His favourite spiritual-ascetic practice is to summon up the horrors of damnation and Hell. The things to be constantly kept in mind are death, the Day of Judgment, Hell and Paradise. Such are the fundamental features of his spiritual asceticism. Nothing should be done without permission. Obedience is the chief virtue. The theatre is unseemly for Christians. Bliss divorces spirit and soul. One should surround oneself with sacred objects. To this a particular significance is attached. All passions must be repudiated, but not civil and family life. It is characteristic of St. Feofan that, although he condemns as temptation all spiritual culture, science, art, all human creation, he blesses the occupation of commerce, middle-class economy and family life, and in particular the authority of the State. This is the reverse of an ascetic renunciation of the world. In Russian Orthodox asceticism there were manifestations akin to the new spirituality preached by Dostoievsky's Elder Zossima. There were also obscurantist manifestations like that of Father Serapion in the *Brothers Karamazov*. They are limited, purely formal expressions of asceticism. Asceticism is undeniably full of dangers. It may lead to an enslavement rather than a liberation of man's spiritual forces. It was often merely on opportunist compromise with evil and unjust actuality, a refusal to come to grips with it.

Asceticism is what man can do. He can practise abstinence, he can fast, he can be continent, he can distribute his wealth among his fellow-men, he can limit his necessities. He can attempt to do this at any time. But the gift of love, the mystical experience of communion with God and the other world, the vision of heavenly light, all these things do not depend on him alone. Mysticism as opposed to asceticism does not emanate from man alone; it supposes the agency of Divine grace, the influence of spirit on man. The *pneuma*, like a breath of evening wind, blows upon man and transforms him. It is sometimes said that through asceticism man ascends to God, but that in mysticism God reveals Himself in man. A distinction should also be made between asceticism and morality. Through asceticism man aspires to perfection, through morality man fulfils a minimum. But it is an error to compare evangelical maximalism with asceticism; they are quite different principles. Evangelical maximalism is a revelation of the Kingdom of God. In it everything is maximal and absolute. Asceticism, on the other hand, takes account of the relativity of human endeavour, of methodical endeavour. And, unlike the Gospel, asceticism has no glad tidings of the Kingdom of God as a completely new life, free from the burden of the world. The Evangel is a revelation of the freedom of spirit and the spiritual life; but asceticism remains the slave of determination. It would be incorrect to explain the evangelical exhortation to bear the Cross, to be self-denying in sacrifice, in terms of asceticism. It is something quite different. The bearing of the Cross is a fundamental mystery in the life of this world; it is neither an ascetic exercise nor a form of self-torture. On the contrary, to bear the Cross is a liberation from the darkness and gloom of the world and of human suffering. It is an illumination, a communion with Christ's ways, not a human principle of salvation. The asceticism which advocated self-torture has turned away from the commandments of the Gospel. The Gospel spirit is radically opposed to any form of utilitarianism or formality such as is to be found in asceticism. The Gospel overcomes the ancient dread of impurity.

When we investigate the psychology of asceticism, we are inevitably confronted with the problem: Are self-inflicted torments and tortures pleasing to God? The belief that man can propitiate God and placate His anger by deliberately and methodically torturing himself is prevalent in asceticism. This is really a Christian version of the ancient pagan belief in the necessity of propitiatory sacrifices to the gods. This nation has left a fatal imprint on the idea even of redemption. This unenlightened belief has nothing in common with the positive interpretation of suffering and sacrifice. In any case asceticism is in need of constant spiritualization and liberation from magic elements. Luther's criticism was in many ways apt and helped to liberate asceticism, although his own notion of the spiritual life was very limited and poor. Luther was convinced that men became monks out of despair, out of fear—for want of another way of salvation. Hence the utilitarian interpretation of good deeds. Luther wished to cast off the burden of sin through faith in Christ. He started out in quest of some guarantee of salvation, but became convinced that such a guarantee could not be found in monastic asceticism. But this did not help him to rise above a utilitarian interpretation of the spiritual life. The same is true of Jansenism with its awe-inspiring God.

III

There are three forms of asceticism: that of fear and reward, that of liberation from the power of the world, and that of disinterested love of God. The first type should be definitely discarded. Asceticism may deal with the body in different ways. It may advocate neglect and mortification of the body, or the training of the body in order to preserve and increase its forces. Vladimir Solovyev maintained that matter separated from God was evil infinity, unquenchable thirst. Thus it would appear that an ascetic dualism of spirit and matter is non-Christian. The

Church was aware of the implication and condemned extreme forms of asceticism and spiritualization. Christianity, unlike Buddhism, requires a domination of flesh rather than a liberation from it. But in the historical Church particular forms of asceticism, and the importance attached to them, depended largely on social influences; and these, in their turn, helped to deform them. It seems parodoxical that the Church should have insisted on a strict and coercive attitude to sex, while at the same time it should have been comparatively indulgent towards sins related to property, covetousness, gain, and the economic exploitation of men. Communion was denied to those who did not conform with the established forms of sexual life—forms which were determined by changing social conditions. In Catholicism there are many tragic cases where communion was refused to those whose bond was not socially approved, although founded on a lofty and authentic love. This is a disgraceful form of Pharisaic legalism. The Church was less severe in the case of the most shameful lust of all, that of property and gain, of oppressed poverty and exploited labour. The Gospel is, of course, no less categorical in its renunciation of property. The question may well be asked: Which is nearer the original sin, *concupiscentia*, the sin of the flesh, or an offence against fellow-men, against human dignity, a condemnation of men to penury and hunger? But the Church had fallen into the hands of the governing classes, and therefore its hierarchy was unable to put into practice the commandments about property. The Church could not refuse communion to those who exploited their fellow-beings economically instead of serving them. Having welded the family to property the Church concentrated on the sexual problem. It is better to repent for having offended a fellow-being in social life, than for having broken a fast or for having failed to observe an ascetic vow.

Does asceticism help to illuminate human nature or to expand the human consciousness? Experience does not confirm the

positive affirmations of ascetic theory. The asceticism of renunciation fails completely to illuminate the whole man, all the dark
recesses of human nature. A monk may spend twenty years of
his life in a cell, diligently practise ascetic exercises, give up the
greater part of his day to prayer, and still be involved in the
deepest obscurantism as regards the ethical values of social life.
Bishop Feofan the Hermit was such an obscurantist. And so were
many of the Fathers. Even in the life of the saints there is only a
partial illumination of human nature. The views held by St.
Seraphim of Sarov about the Western cult, politics and culture,
were very unillumined, although the heart of his being was
radiant. Thus asceticism can fail to enlighten the mind; and in
any case, enlightenment of this kind cannot be the automatic
result of any asceticism, however consistent and sincere. Asceticism, considered solely as a method, should help the liberation of
man's creative forces. But actually it has had the contrary effect,
that of extinguishing man's creative nature. This gives rise to the
problem of the relation between asceticism and inspiration.
Inspiration alone develops the positive side of human nature and
frees it from the burden of sin. In so far as it is hostile to inspiration,
asceticism fails to illuminate man. Inspiration is a breath of spirit:
man's interpenetration by spirit, by the *pneuma*. That is, indeed,
the source of every creative fact. Asceticism bears a dual relation
to inspiration: on the one hand it can concentrate and direct man's
creative forces; on the other it can kill man's creative forces by
regarding inspiration as sinful. Actually, asceticism has mostly
been negative. Man's inherent erotic power can be concentrated,
purified and directed to creative ends or sublimated. But this
erotic element inherent in inspiration and creativeness may also
be eliminated, suppressed and killed. Asceticism is an enemy of
inspiration and the creative *Eros*; it aspires to eradicate man's
human content. The result is an emasculation of human nature.
This type of asceticism fails to bring about the revelation of the
Divine image in man. In the writings of the Holy Fathers it was

said that virtue was created of the same material as the passions. From each passion a corresponding virtue must be formed. But asceticism too often extinguishes or deadens the passions, thus annihilating the material source of the virtues. There is nothing more repulsive than petrified lifeless virtues, than an ascetic turned mummy, become an enemy of all human impulses. It is usually argued that inspiration is dangerous, as love and all creativeness are dangerous. That obedience and meekness alone are harmless, is an illusion, and a self-delusion, of a false asceticism which makes man its victim. There is no sphere, however restricted or guarded, in which man would be justified in considering himself safe and secure. The spiritual life is highly dangerous and full of risks. There is evidence for this in the descriptions of the most remarkable psychic experience of humanity. Trials and tribulations are the lot especially of spiritual men. Comparative security is the privilege of simple shopkeepers. Man's dignity as a free spirit is closely associated with trials, temptations, dangers and risks. The very search for safety and security is an evil temptation of the religious life, a falsehood, a self-delusion. The development of spirituality should be accompanied by increasing dangers rather than by security. Only the middle classes seek a secure, solid and assured foundation in religion. Obedience and meekness may also have their dangers, and in their worse sense they may even prove to be more dangerous than inspiration and creativeness. Obedience can easily become servitude, an abdication of responsibility, a betrayal of spirit, of freedom, of the God-man. Obedience can become an instrument of evil. Meekness can assume all the characteristics of pride. The pride of the meek is the worst kind of pride. Meekness may also quite easily turn into hypocrisy. It manifests itself in a conventional and rhetorical manner, which has no relation to reality or any kind of sincerity. The gestures, words, expressions of meekness can all be revolting. Inspiration, the creative breath of spirit, alone can preserve man from this dangerous distortion of his image. The fear of inspiration and creativeness is itself a sin born of a slavish and perverted interpretation of sin. But actually this false obsession with sin is instilled by human egocentricity and selfishness, by man's inability to achieve real liberation and renunciation. Egocentricity breeds meekness and transforms obedience into self-righteousness.

Through consciousness of sin the problem of asceticism is related to the problem of man. But in its deeper sense the latter is not, as is commonly maintained, merely a problem of a pessimistic or an optimistic attitude to human nature. The traditional forms of asceticism humiliated man. But that is no reason for opposing to them the optimistic doctrine of Jean Jacques Rousseau. Human nature is dual, lofty and base, free and slavish, Godlike and elemental. Human nature is polarized; and that fact influences the whole of man's spiritual life. This dualism is apparent throughout Christian history and assumes the most perverted forms. Christianity ascetically denied the world, but at the same time it adapted itself only too easily to the world. Christian asceticism was the reverse side of its adaptability to the world. There was an ascetic consecration of the worst, the most unjust and slavish forms of worldly life, on the pretext that human nature was sinful and required the repression and suffering of a violent asceticism. Man was conscious of being at the mercy of evil powers. Actually this was merely an objectification of sin, an exteriorization of it. It was an excuse for frightening man. It might prove to be an obstacle to inner concentration, to the renunciation of the external world. Sinfulness was that external thing upon which man was made to depend. Man was encouraged to believe—and he reinforced this belief by auto-suggestion—that he had no spiritual forces capable of resisting sin. Thus sin, and the resistance to it, were both conceived as external forces; whereas actually the agency of the Holy Spirit, without which man could not struggle against sin, belief or hope, is a most sacred and inward force. Spiritual asceticism is concentration, meditation and contemplation. It is an occult inner process, but one also capable of being exteriorized and objectified. In that case the spiritual life is a clash of exterior forces by which man feels himself crushed. Sin displaces the centre of human gravity and makes human nature egocentric. As a result all things appear to be external to man. From the egocentric standpoint, spirituality is something external rather than inward and deep. That is the immanent penalty of egocentricity. For spirit to become an inner force it is essential to lose the sense of egocentricity. This is the paradox of spiritual life. The diabolical, infernal world is a nightmare, a hallucination of the subject, a product of false objectification. Man perceives the nightmare of the diabolical world as an external actuality simply because he fails to transcend himself. False asceticism may encourage this state of affairs rather than deliver man from it. The only justifiable asceticism is that which liberates man and restores him to authentic realities. Asceticism should restore man's dignity, not plunge him into a hopeless state of indignity and baseness. In so far as asceticism secludes man and separates him from his fellow-beings, it plunges him still more into himself and becomes another form of egocentricity. Such is the consequence of concentrating on personal salvation and perdition. But there is need of an asceticism which should educate man to communion and fraternity. Man's destiny is linked up with that of the world; he must bear the burden of the world, he must be creatively active in as well as free from the world. In the contemporary world men are forced to live in a regimented society; they are the slaves of society, but at bottom they remain terribly solitary and lonely. This situation calls for new forms of asceticism. The egocentric degeneration of asceticism assumed a variety of forms. Among others, it could achieve man's salvation by means of his relationships with other men. Even love and charity were interpreted as an ascetic principle of salvation rather than as a real means of transcending self. In asceticism of this kind there is no escape from the Ego, no real communion with the mystery of another's personality. Man remains a closed monad, seeking his own salvation. But man is not a monad, but a microcosm. This type of asceticism is destined to disappear. Contemporary man has need of a different kind of asceticism, of concentration, of renunciation, of a limitation of growing necessities and their infinite longing. The foundations must be laid of this new asceticism as well as of a new spirituality. The ontological justification of asceticism is its achievement of simplicity or wholeness, of freedom from complexity or disintegration. But the achievement of Divine simplicity implies not the annihilation of the complex world, but its illumination and transfiguration, its integration in a higher unity. This will involve the appearance of a new type of saint, who will take upon himself the burden of the complex world.

CHAPTER V

EVIL AND SUFFERING AS PROBLEMS OF SPIRIT

I

Asceticism is intimately related to an awareness of sin and the struggle waged against it. Sin gives birth to suffering. By practising asceticism man inflicted voluntary suffering on himself in order to counteract the effects of externally imposed suffering. Asceticism was a means by which men hoped to overcome evil. The whole of the spiritual life is bound up with the theme of evil and suffering. Thus pessimism played an important part in stimulating the development of spiritual currents. The enemies of spirit, of the religious life, attempted in this way to compromise the very genesis of spirituality and faith in the spiritual world. If there were no suffering, if man were not humiliated and impotent, then there would be no spirituality as a transcending force in the life of this world, no birth of faith in the transcendent world. Epicurus has already attributed the origin of religious beliefs to fear, thus failing to grasp that fear was an even deeper phenomenon than he had imagined. Kierkegaard had the best understanding of the profound nature of fear or terror. Feuerbach, and then Marx, attempted to compromise every religious belief and every spiritualism. According to them, the belief in the transcendental world, in spirituality, was merely an abstraction of human nature, a source of weakness and unhappiness for man. Unhappy, powerless man had an almighty God. A strong and happy man will have no need of God any more; he will recover the plenitude of abstracted nature. But this new plenitude will dispense with spirituality; man will finally be a terrestrial, self-sufficient and material creature. Spirituality depended on the

G

abstraction of human nature, on its transposition into a supra-human illusory sphere. Spirituality was the source of suffering, unhappiness, and an escape into unreality. A real victory over suffering and unhappiness would mean the end of spirituality as a mystification of the consciousness. Spirituality was a diseased product of suffering.

In this criticism of spirituality, its connection with suffering and evil was correctly grasped. But truth and reality are the very reverse of what Feuerbach, Marx and later antispiritualists supposed. Far from being an abstraction of human nature, an illusion of consciousness, spirituality is man's innermost dwelling-place, the very source of his being. It is, on the contrary, materialism which abstracts and does violence to human nature. Capitalism, in which Marx beheld such an abstraction of human nature, is materialism. The greatest of all rationalistic illusions is that ultimate deliverance from human suffering and unhappiness will be realized in the external sphere of organized life. That is, in fact, a form of human abstraction. Human happiness cannot be organized; nor can life's tragic contradictions, human fatality, death, be rationally and technically controlled; nor can the essential mystery of life be resolved. But the attempt has been made to abstract in the external and social sphere the whole problem of man and eternity, the human personality, and the objective world. To avoid any misunderstanding, I at once proclaim the need to resolve and to do away with such human misfortunes and sufferings as are associated with monstrous social inequalities, man's bitter necessities and slavery. Social injustice, man's exploitation of man are evils which can be repaired. This can be achieved through the reorganization of human society. But this will not end but rather intensify the tragedy of life; it will promote an even greater nostalgia, and even a more intense spirituality—hitherto kept in check by external misfortunes and a badly organized society—will manifest itself. Man will rebel against final objectification. He will make an effort to preserve his inwardness, his profound awareness. Thus in this world, spirituality ever preserves its connection with the experience of suffering, with the contradictions and conflicts of human existence, with the hostile facts of death and eternity. There is nothing spiritual or even human about a completely happy and contented creature, impervious to evil, suffering pain and tragedy. A sensitive awareness of evils and a capacity for suffering are one of the attributes of the spiritual man. Man is a creature who suffers and feels compassion, who is sensitive to pity, who in these ways proves the dignity of human nature. Hence man seeks deliverance not only in the outer but also in the inner world, not only in the social but also in the spiritual sphere. And his longing to be delivered from society and mediocrity may be even more intense than his longing to escape the suffering caused by tragic contradictions in the world. Man's spiritual history is a search for inner deliverance both from his own suffering and that of the world. This accounts for the great importance of religions proclaiming deliverance. Thus it is that human dignity and man's vocation for eternity are spoken of in pessimistic rather than in optimistic philosophies. But the teleological conception of life discovers the existence of another world, of God, and insists on the evil state and suffering of the world. If all things had a uniform goal, if the tragic contradictions of life were abolished, if there were an end to suffering, then man would lose the power of transcending himself and his urge to do so. But it becomes apparent that logical pessimism and logical optimism are both equally passive attitudes. Either everything is hopeless and unchangeably bad, or everything is steadily improving. An actively creative attitude to life is superior to both pessimism and optimism. The suffering of human life does not depend entirely on necessity or the inevitability of natural laws, it depends even more on accident. Chance is a tremendous factor in human destiny. For the most part man is obliged to attribute his fortune or misfortune to chance—to an irrational and inexplicable element acting independently of all laws. A particular *combination of circumstances* revealed in chance is not determined by any special laws governing man's fortune or misfortune. It is a serious error to interpret chance as an expression of a universal will directing life towards a uniform goal. Our spiritual attitude to chance—the source of so many of our misfortunes—should admit its objective expediency but regard it as a problem intended to test our spiritual awareness. The significance of *unfortunate accidents* lies in the trial of our spiritual strength, in the subjective rather than the objective sphere. From the objective standpoint universal life has no purpose, but the task of spirit is to infuse it with purpose.

History provides us with eternal images of unjust suffering and of the injustice of human destinies. The phenomenon of unjust suffering is of especial importance to the spiritual life, for through it we are brought into contact with the depths of existence. The story of Job is in a way symbolical of terrestrial human destiny. The ancient Hebrews had a peculiar conviction that the blessings of life and happiness were the reward of a virtuous life. If the blessings of life were withheld from man, if he were unhappy, then clearly this was a sign that his virtue had faltered and he had transgressed. Reward and punishment were meted out to man in this terrestrial life. In the light of this notion it was difficult to conceive the idea of *unjust* punishment. That was the dilemma in which Job's comforters found themselves. Job was a pious and virtuous man; he always respected God and was obedient to His Law. But nevertheless the blessings of life were withheld from him; he became the unhappiest of mortals afflicted with unbear-,able sufferings. His comforters did their best to justify the expediency of his unhappy fate. But Job was adamant. He rebelled against God and wrestled with Him, invoking the Divine sense of justice. God justified Job and condemned his comforters. Our world is full of Job's comforters, full of such friends. Men find it very difficult not to think in terms of expediency, and therefore the notion of *unjust suffering* is for them hard to grasp. Many jump to the conclusion that the existence of unjust suffering postulates the non-existence of God or of a Divine Providence. That is one of the arguments, perhaps the strongest, of atheism. The world is full of Jobs—big or little. And, like Job's comforters, we are unwilling to sympathize with their sufferings. Take, for example, the fate of Socrates, the wisest, the most virtuous, and the most just of the Greeks. He was condemned to death, made to drink poison, by his people. In his remarkable article on Plato, Vladimir Solovyev states that the death of Socrates, his master, had a determining influence on Plato's vision. Plato renounced the plural sensible world, *this world*, in which such a fate could be meted out to a great and just man. In such a world there could be no justice, purpose, good or truth. And so Plato turned towards the world of ideas, the supra-sensible world, and sought therein the supreme blessing—good. Greek tragedy had already portrayed types of unjust sufferers. The tragic hero was, in fact, such a type. There was no personal guilt attaching to Oedipus, but only the burden of fatality. In the world of Greek tragedy there was no one to whom an appeal could be addressed as Job had invoked God the Almighty. The only solution of Greek tragedy was in an aesthetic truce with fate, *amor fati*. The world was full of gods, but they themselves were subordinate to fate. In his vision of another world, of a world of eternal ideas, Plato attempted to escape from the immanent whirlpool of cosmic fatality. In this ideal world there was a supreme good. But Plato was unable to escape from dualism. The world of ideas could neither change nor save the plural sensible world.

But the history of the world can provide the example of a more overwhelming destiny that that of Job, Socrates, or the great majority of men. That is the fate and crucifixion of Jesus of Nazareth. It is not necessary to be a devout Christian to believe that Jesus of Nazareth was the greatest of saints, the most sinless of all men. With the exception of a few elect no one recognized Him; He was repudiated, condemned to a shameful death and crucified. This event epitomized all the sufferings of the world, all human suffering. Thus *unjust suffering*, that of a just man, was transformed into a mystery—a mystery of salvation. Therein unjust suffering appeared in another light—as seen from on high. It was not only the most just of men who was thus crucified, but also the Son of God. Unjust suffering was Divine suffering. And unjust Divine suffering proved to be an expiation of all human suffering. The world was in the power of evil: it repudiated the greatest of all saints; it crucified Him, the Divine Son; it crucified God Himself. The crucifixion of the Divine Son was a response to human suffering and the evil of the world. The fate of Jesus Christ was enacted in sight of the evilly-intentioned world, and of the unjustly persecuted and humiliated. Evil manifests itself in a dual way in the world: through the dark evil will of the crucifiers and through the unjust suffering of the crucified. Evil is both the cause of injustice, falsehood and suffering and the endurance of that injustice, falsehood and suffering. Hence the boundless difficulty of any attempt to grasp the agency of Divine Providence in the world. A rationalistic interpretation of Divine Providence must inevitably lead to the denial of evil—to an attitude similar to that of Job's comforters. A rationalistic theodicy in the manner of Leibnitz culminates in an atheistic revolt, in a negation of God. The mystery of the Cross, the crucifixion of God Himself, was a temptation in the opinion of the Jews, madness in that of the Hellenists. The world is in the power of evil; it is a fallen world, the product of original sin. In this world there is no apparent rational and moral uniformity of goal. There are, instead, irreconcilable good and evil, unjust suffering, the tragic destiny of great and just men. It is a world in which prophets are stoned and unjust men, the persecutors and crucifiers of the just, are triumphant. It is a world in which innocent children and innocent animals have to suffer. It is a world in which death, evil and suffering reign supreme. Is Divine Providence effective in this world? That is the question of reason—meaningless when confronted with the mystery and secret of love. Suffering is also a mystery and secret. Suffering is a mystery because it can also become expiation. We are confronted with the most torturing problem of the human consciousness and conscience—the problem of the origin of evil in a divinely created world. The spiritual life is beset with its own suffering and that of other men. Suffering is associated with guilt, with ancient primordial guilt. But there is also unjust suffering. If I can live through—and even then not always—my suffering as a penance, then the experience of another's suffering can easily make of me a Job's comforter or, even worse, one of those who crucified Christ. That is the fundamental paradox of suffering and of the Cross. It is part of the mystery of pity and love. That paradox implies a dual attitude to suffering. From the remotest times man has longed to be delivered from the intolerable burden of suffering and from servitude to evil. Man's greatest spiritual flights are associated with this longing. Men of the highest standing in the human hierarchy, men of royal blood like Sakya-Muni, like Marcus Aurelius, have given tentative answers to the torturing problem of evil and suffering; and so have men of humble position like the slave Epictetus, like the carpenter Jesus, who gave a Divine answer to this problem.

In the history of pre-Christian spirituality the most interesting statements of the problem were made by Buddhism, Stoicism, Orphism and Neo-Platonism. At this point I shall be obliged to go over some of the ground already covered in the chapter on asceticism. The renouncement of the personality is one of the ways of seeking deliverance from suffering and evil. This is even a predominant form within Christianity. In Buddhism this idea was radically expanded to include a total renunciation of being. Our understanding of Hindu philosophy and Oriental thought in general is imperfect, because these philosophies were elaborated independently of the Greek and European traditions. In our attempt to comprehend them we have a tendency to translate them into the categories of Western thought. Hence, to me at least, the nature of the Buddhist *nirvana* appears problematic. It is probably extraneous to the distinction between being and non-being. But its significance can be partly grasped by analogy with *apophatic* knowledge. Buddhism indentifies being and suffering. Evil is also suffering. The realization of this truth, that *being is suffering*, is already a step towards deliverance from suffering, from the bitterness of being. It is salvation through knowledge—self-salvation. Thus Buddhism dispenses with a saviour. It is a debatable point whether Buddhism can be included in the category of atheistic religion. It represents rather an *apophatic* form of pantheism or acosmism. Buddhism is afraid of suffering and renounces the human personality in order to be delivered from suffering. The amazing and touching thing about Buddhism is its sensitivity to human suffering, the great compassion it feels not only for man but for all animals and living creatures. That is the great virtue of Buddhism. But Buddhism knows only compassion but not love; it is spiritually cold and ignores the warmth of the human heart. Love implies election; it is exclusive, lofty, and intimately related to the mystery of the personality. Compassion and charity, which may be extended to all living creatures, come down from above to a suffering and, as it were, God-forsaken world. Love is an eternal affirmation of the being of the human personality. Buddhism abstains from such an affirmation. It regards personal being as phantasmal, as a source of suffering. In this sense, both Schopenhauer and Tolstoy had affinities with Buddhism; and Tolstoy's spirituality in particular has an impersonal character. Stoicism also bears certain formal affinities to Buddhism, although it originated in an entirely different world. Stoics are not so sensitive to suffering, nor do they renounce being. But they aim first of all at deliverance from suffering rather than at a transformation of the world. If Buddhism tends to be pessimistic, then Stoicism is an original blend of pessimism in life and an extreme cosmic optimism. Stoicism advocates deliverance from the sufferings and evils of the world through a harmony of human life with universal reason, the cosmic Logos and harmony. For the Stoics, deliverance is associated with a change of attitude to events. Everything depends on the attitude of the human consciousness. Every event, even the most painful one, can turn out to be propitious. It is a question of being able to achieve a dispassionate, apathetic state. Man should train himself to be contemptous of and indifferent to everything external, to treat dispassionately everything that pains him. Stoic spirituality is attuned to the world as it is. Buddhism, on the other hand, regards the world as a mirage and phantom to be dissipated at will. The Stoics believed in a world governed by reason, in the necessity of wise indifference to the causes of suffering and death itself. Stoicism was the spiritual manifestation of a world already on the brink of dissolution and prescient of its own imminent doom. But Stoicism also contained an element of universal humanism which exalted it above ancient consciousness as a whole. It was a presentiment, as it were, of coming Christianity.

One of the ways of deliverance is to transcend the limitations of the individuality, to merge and unite with the impersonal cosmic elements. That is the way of Orgiasm, of the Dionysian cults. Briefly, such is the cosmic mysticism of the pagan world. The personality is delivered from suffering and evil by reuniting with the primal elements. It would be more correct to state that the personality had not yet really awakened or become aware of itself. There is nothing surprising in the fact that man sought deliverance by renouncing his personal existence, by transcending the limitations and the forms of the personality. For personality implies pain, and its realization brings suffering. The labour of engendering the personality implies sacrifice, but not the renunciation of the personality. But oblivion and salvation were the aim of the Orgiastic and Dionysiac cults. This experience lacked human control, humanity itself; it was a form of Divine bestiality. In it the elemental depths of man triumphed over the personal human element, over the Apollonian principle. But this

Dionysian elementalism, this source of tragedy, also helped to contribute to human plenitude. An exclusive reliance on the Apollonian principle leads to formalism and finality. In Greece, Orphism was the true religion of deliverance and salvation. The barbaric Dionysian elementalism, which was Thracian rather than Greek in origin, was transformed and given a new direction by Orphism. The mystical Dionysian element persisted, but the human image was no longer disrupted in Orgiastic delirium. The interest of Orphism lies chiefly in its revelation of Greek pessimism, in its pessimistic interpretation of the world. It conceived a world submerged in sin from which man longed to escape. Orphism had also a peculiar sense of ancient guilt. Man was a dual being torn between a Divine inspired element and an evil, tellurgic, Titanic element. In the beginning of the world there was the crime of the Titans, from which man's Divine nature sought deliverance. The soul was a prisoner of the material world, of the body, and longed to be set free and to return to its spiritual home. Orphism exercised a tremendous influence on Greek philosophy in general and Plato in particular. The problem of evil was formulated thus by the Greeks: Evil is born of matter, which is the *meon*. Deliverance from evil is deliverance from matter, a separation of the higher principle from the lower. The Divine element in man is essentially an intellectual element (*nous*) and should be separated from matter. The higher principle does not transfigure the lower; it simply abstracts itself from it, abandoning it to the *meonic* state. This conception had a definite repercussion on Neo-Platonic spirituality and Gnosticism. As we have already noted, Plotinus had explained the origin of evil as a material mixture, necessitating an almost mechanical severance of man's higher nature—in itself sinless and pure—from the composite body, thus achieving man's liberation from evil and his deliverance from suffering. This constituted an original blend of monism and dualism. Thus the source of evil was material rather than spiritual. But Orphism as well as Neo-Platonism had a profound sense of the sorrow of existence, of evil and suffering in the world, of the need for deliverance. In Neo-Platonism deliverance was achieved through the intellect; in Gnosticism it was achieved through knowledge. But deliverance was also sought for in the mysteries. Thus the theme of evil had been propounded. It was a torturing problem for Marcion, for the Gnostics, for the Manichees. Human thought fluctuates between monism and dualism. Thus the problem of evil is the definitive mystery; and a new spirituality cannot ignore it.

II

Whence comes evil? And how shall we live if evil be so great? That is the problem confronting every conscious man who has advanced a stage beyond the merely vegetable and animal life. The development of consciousness is also a development of the *unhappy consciousness*, as Hegel called it. And it must, indeed, be admitted that consciousness does make man unhappy. From this state of unhappy consciousness, of awareness of evil and suffering, man attempts either to return to the subconscious or to attain the superconscious. Consciousness is not whole but divided. Wholeness is peculiar to the subconscious or to the superconscious. The development of consciousness and that of spirituality are not one and the same thing. Consciousness reflects the state of the world, and is often bewildered by it.

In fact the wicked world disrupts consciousness and prevents it from grasping the significance of evil. The development of spirituality implies a passage beyond disrupted consciousness towards superconsciousness, an escape from the power of necessity, from the casual world, into a sphere of freedom and love. Growing spirituality liberates the human soul from the power of evil and illuminates the human consciousness. But evil remains the most serious problem of human existence. Suffering is not evil but is caused by it. If there were no suffering in this wicked world, then very likely there would be no acuity of consciousness or growth of spirituality. Inability to suffer sometimes proves to be the greatest evil of all. Dostoievsky maintained that suffering was the unique *raison d'être* of the consciousness. Philosophical thought has paid too little attention to the problem of evil, modern thought even less than ancient. Nevertheless many attempts have been made to solve the problem of the origin of evil. These attempts, however, were usually based upon a conjunction of philosophical and religious thought. Any rationalized approach to the problem, even when it takes the form of a theological doctrine based on revelation, leads to the abolition of the problem, of mystery, and ultimately to a simple justification or negation of evil. But evil is entirely irrational and without foundation, quite undetermined by any purpose or reason. It is useless to inquire into the origin of evil, because it is engendered by the world of necessity in which everything is subordinated to causality. But evil is initially related to freedom rather than to causality. It seems paradoxical, but there is an affinity between evil and spirit. They have a common attribute in freedom, although evil, of course, is destructive to both spirit and freedom. It is true that evil originates from spirit rather than matter. To say that freedom is the cause of evil is the same as saying that evil has no cause. In this case freedom does mean absence of cause. It is only at a later stage, in its consequences that evil submits to the power of causality. Evil may be a cause, but it has itself no cause. Freedom is a definite mystery, an irrational element. It engenders evil as well as good without any discrimination, content simply to engender. There can be no rational interpretation of freedom; a rational definition would only kill freedom. That is known as a definitive conception (*Grenzbegriff*). Thus evil is born of freedom, it has neither cause nor foundation.

In exactly the same way we cannot speak of God as a cause; nor is the Divine Agency a cause operating on the consequences engendered by it. This helps to throw some light also on the Divine tragedy. The Divine tragedy becomes a Divine comedy when made dependent on a system of thought in which everything proceeds from on high, from God—and is comprehended by Him. This is the case of systems like Platonism, Neo-Platonism and, finally, Thomism. Everything emanates from the One, from God, and descends towards the plural world and then ascendingly returns from the plural world to the One, to God. Such are the monistic systems. In spite of all the complexities introduced by Christianity, the official rational systems of Christian theology are as monistic as the system of Plotinus. All things emanate exclusively from the Godhead. Thus the Almighty and Omniscient God is constantly confronted with Himself, His appeals are answered not by others but by Himself. There is no dual communion, no dialogical struggle. In this context, evil must necessarily be determined by God, the First Cause of evil as well as of all things; and in the external world there is only the agency of secondary and derivative causes. The irrational mystery of freedom ceases to exist. The irrational mystery of freedom independent of Divine creation and determination does not imply the existence of another being claiming equality with Divine Being, it does not in the least imply an ontological dualism. A dualism of this sort would involve rationalization. Freedom postulated as the spontaneous origin of evil, as well as of everything new in the world, is not the elaboration of any ontological or metaphysical doctrine, but an intuitive description of the mystery revealed in existence. Freedom exposes the limitations of every kind of rational thought; it appears irrational, abysmal, without foundations, inexplicable, non-objectifiable. It is revealed in human existence, in spiritual experience. It is a refutation of the rationalized theological doctrines of the origin of evil. The mystery of freedom contains both the mystery of evil and that of creation. This gives birth to the Divine tragedy, the dual communion, the dialogical struggle, the answer given by man to God. Jacob Boehme's *Ungrund* is that very freedom. It is impossible to formulate a conception of *Ungrund*; it is a myth and symbol, the limit of any rationalization. Evil cannot, indeed, be interpreted conceptionally, but only mythologically and symbolically. A monistic system of concepts in which everything emanates from on high obscures the irrational mystery of evil and the irrational secret of creating the hitherto non-existent. Every system of concepts, every theological system, is governed by causal categorical thought, by necessity and determinism. In the light of this, attempts are made to explain the origins of evil and freedom. God is conceived as a universal, all-comprehending cause. In his doctrine of the intelligible character and freedom, Kant was perhaps nearer the truth than other philosophers, although he did draw false conclusions from his premises. Evil and suffering exist because freedom exists; but freedom has no foundation of existence, it is a frontier. But because freedom exists, God Himself suffers and is crucified. The Divine love and sacrifice are an answer to the mystery of freedom wherein evil and suffering have their origin. Divine love and sacrifice are likewise freedom.

It is difficult for man to reconcile himself to the injustice and gratuitousness of the sufferings that befall him. Man is capable of enduring a great deal, of enduring sufferings which at first appear unbearable. But the hardest thing of all to endure is gratuitous suffering. Man's whole being revolts against such sufferings. Too many people on earth believe that their sufferings are unjust; they fail to understand why they in particular should be afflicted with torturing diseases, bitter need, failures, betrayals, why they should be made to suffer more than other men who are no better and who are in many cases worse than they are. The original sin is no explanation of human misfortunes because it refers to a *general* rather than a *particular* state. The more fortunate and successful of men are nevertheless quite as bewildered by original sin. If we attempt to work out the proportion between suffering and sin, we become Job's comforters. It is impossible to rationalize human destiny. If we should attempt to do so, that would involve us in a justification of everything and, in fact, in a negation of the istence of evil. The problem of spiritual life does not consist in explaining or justifying the sufferings of life, but in illuminating and spiritually surviving them. The burden of the Cross is such a spiritually illuminating experience of suffering. Man should bear his own Cross in life and help other men to bear theirs. The notion that every suffering is deserved, and is a just consequence of sin, can lead to a conception of life diametrically opposed to that propounded in the Gospel commandments of love and charity. There are austere ascetics and puritans who are predominantly unfavourable and censorious in their attitude to their fellow-men. They have no wish to lighten the burden of human suffering, which they regard as a just punishment.

Man's attitude to suffering is always dual and paradoxical, and there can be no rational solution to this. A spiritual attitude implies illumination, or a vital knowledge of the meaning of suffering and a sense of liberation. The development of spirituality is a sure sign that man has not been crushed by suffering. The acceptance of the Cross is at the same time an alleviation of suffering, for it assumes a purpose in the spiritual life. A refusal to take up the burden of the Cross, a repudiation of suffering, makes of suffering a dark and incalculable force. Thus there are two kinds of suffering: a dark suffering leading to perdition and an illumined suffering leading to salvation. But an admitted purpose in suffering should not imply a negation of the existence of evil and injustice, or a negation of man's struggle for a less torturing and more joyful life. On the contrary, in society it is necessary to oppose unjust suffering and to abstain from hypocritical sermons justifying the suffering of the unfortunate. The contemplation of suffering can easily breed hypocrisy. My experience of suffering as a fulfilment of purpose is the way of spiritualization and illumination, is my spiritual experience rather than a rational justification of suffering. We shall never understand why one man is so unhappy while another seems so happy—I say *seems*, because there are no very happy men but only moments of happiness. Man's entire life, from the hour of his birth to that of his death, is but a day of life torn from the whole, infinite and external life. The events of a single day, sometimes very important events, are incomprehensible when regarded independently of preceding and succeeding days. And so it is with the whole of man's life. The doctrine of metempsychosis is an attempt to rationalize the mystery of human destiny, and it may appear to be a more satisfactory and reassuring doctrine than many others. But it involves a denial of injustice and evil in human life and a belief in an all-embracing chain of causality, moral as well as natural. But the significance of suffering does not consist in the fact that it is necessary and just or is the supreme law of life, but in the fact that it is an experience of freedom and of the path along which man travels, in the course of which he may realize his spiritual victory, achieve liberation and illumination, fulfil the covenant of love and charity. Man is not only sinful or determined by his evil past, he is also profoundly unhappy. And for that reason only compassion, pity and love have a metaphysical significance. There is nothing more false than to attribute causality to justice, than to insinuate a moral purpose into determination. As a correlative we have the false interpretation of the agency of Divine Providence in this world. Causality is not the only reason why evil, injustice and unjust suffering exist in the world; freedom is another reason, because it has a certain tendency to become inevitable causality.

III

Evil is not most disturbing and painful when it is manifest, but when it is disguised as good. In world history evil for the most part assumes the appearance of good. Good only too frequently turns out to be evil. This was often the case of Christian good. In this category we can place Pharisaism, legality, hypocrisy, conventional rhetoric, and the crystallization of the notion of 'goodness' in bourgeois society. The bourgeois state is a spiritual category only in the sense in which it is a negation and a falsification of spirit. The history of the world as a whole has a fatal tendency to relapse into a bourgeois state. Christianity, spiritual philosophy, Socialism, revolution, all revert sooner or later to bourgeois stability. The bourgeois state is the end of the creative spiritual impulse, the extinction and death of fire. The bourgeois makes use of the creative achievements of spirit. To further his ends he will not disdain any great symbol of the past. He does not believe in the world of invisible things, and does not venture to associate his destiny with that world. He believes in the world of perceptible things; and this is the world which he builds and consolidates, and with which his destiny is irremediably bound. He has transformed Christianity into a conservative, visible institution. He fears anything in the nature of uncertainty or a problem. He lives in perpetual fear that his assured and peaceful existence will be abrogated. He has evolved for his use a special type of spirituality which is not at all spiritual. A voluminous myopic literature has grown up to lull him in false security. The reign of the bourgeois is essentially of *this world*. It is a state to which all things gravitate as if fulfilling a universal law. All the spiritual currents of the world, all revolutionary movements, are drawn towards this stability. This was first of all the case, the tragic destiny of Christianity itself. Its spiritual values were made use of to bolster and safeguard the bourgeois order. Fear made its spirituality an instrument for inspiring fear. The legal normative order of life, bereft of any spirituality, was proclaimed to be the spiritual order. Spirituality was also made the excuse for oppressing the human personality, for subordinating it to false, general and abstract values. All revolutionary movements are anti-bourgeois in their motives, but their victories over the old order have always been marked by the foundation of a new bourgeois state. The French Revolution gave birth to the bourgeois Capitalist world, and the Socialist and Communist revolution will, in its turn, create a new bourgeois world. It might even be said that the reign of the bour-

H

geois is being consolidated more than ever throughout the world, extending its sway and becoming universal. The Middle Ages were the least bourgeois. It is an error to associate the bourgeois state with a particular class—with the Capitalist class, for example, although it is most forcibly expressed in this class. The bourgeoisie has primarily a spiritual rather than a social connotation. There is a bourgeoisie of all classes: that of the nobility, of the peasantry, of the intelligentsia, of the clergy, of the proletariat. The abolition of all class differences, which is a socially desirable thing, will in all probability result in the reign of a universal bourgeoisie. Democracy is one of the ways in which the bourgeois mentality crystallizes itself. In France the bourgeois democracy is more corrupt; in Switzerland it is more virtuous; but it is difficult to say which is the worse. Social life tends invariably towards a bourgeois existence, bourgeois ideas and a fettering of spirit.

Bourgeois life is dominated by money and social position. Another of its characteristics is a complete disregard of the human personality. It is the aim of Socialism to break the monopoly of money and to organize society on a foundation of labour. In that lies its justification. But money is the symbol of worldly power; it would no doubt reappear in some new form in the new Socialist bourgeois state, and man would once more be judged according to his social position. The bourgeoisie is the fortress of virtues, principles, patriotism, family, property, Church, State, morality. It can also be the champion of freedom, equality and fraternity. But such falsehood and falsification are a most terrible manifestation of universal evil. The devil is a liar. Thus a negation of spirit may masquerade itself as a defence of spirit, atheism may assume the form of piety, a contempt for freedom and equality may manifest itself as a championship of them. *Ideas* and *principles* may prove to be a greater evil than desires and immediate instincts. Utilitarianism is a sure sign of bourgeois life; it is the desire to realize something at any cost, to safeguard man by any means. In this way revolutions are also fated to relapse into a bourgeois state, in this way Communism will be transformed and consolidated. In this way the triumph of Christianity, its need to defend its acquisitions, led to its decline in bourgeois society. The rule of the bourgeoisie is opposed to that of spirit and spirituality, which are disinterested and free from social ambitions. Sincerity, authenticity and a familiarity with the original source of life, in the sense intended by Carlyle, are all opposed to the bourgeois mentality. The latter is of social origin; it implies the supremacy of society over man, over his unique and original personality, the tyranny of public opinion and public morality. The bourgeoisie is the rule of social life, of the majority, of the objectification stifling human existence. This mentality is manifest in all spheres—in science, in art, in all forms of human creativeness. The nineteenth century can claim some remarkable men who rebelled against the bourgeois mentality, among them Carlyle, Kierkegaard, Nietzsche, Léon Bloy, Tolstoy and Dostoievsky. They propounded the problem in a more profound way than did the social revolutionaries. They grasped the fact that the problem of spirit was involved. The spiritual life is an escape from social life, a means of overcoming bourgeois tyranny, the finite sphere, the fear of infinity and eternity. The spiritual path leads away from the finite world; it aspires to infinity and eternity, to plenitude as opposed to limitation. The spiritual life is fraught with dangers; it is in no sense a safe life. Spirit will refuse to be a servant of number, mass or conservative interests. Spirit is essentially revolutionary while the mass is reactionary. Spirit is independent of natural reflection and perception, and in this way it has an affinity with magic freedom. It must struggle against the bourgeois evil, against Pharisaic virtues, against high principles. There are two types of bourgeois: the solid type, fortified by principles and morality, who imposes his views on the world and occupies a leading social position—it may be represented by a monk or ascetic, an academician, a proprietor, a ruler; and there is also the frivolous type, the wastrel who enjoys non-being. But the bourgeois is at bottom an optimist;

he believes in happiness solidly achieved in a finite world; he inclines to pessimism only when it is a question of relieving other people's misfortunes and sufferings, of improving the social condition of the workers. The bourgeois usually thinks that the unfortunate are responsible for their misery, and that the fortunate deserve their happiness. We should, of course, adopt a contrary attitude: we should feel optimistic about the improvement of social conditions, and pessimistic about the metaphysical problems of human existence. But the bourgeois refuses to see the tragic element in life. And such is also the outlook of the bourgeois Socialist. The bourgeois attempts to deal with the problem of suffering by suppressing man's inner life and objectifying, as far as possible, human existence. The bourgeois also arrives at a state of apathy, but not of Stoic apathy, towards human suffering.

Existence in the wicked world is a paradox for our spiritual life —a paradox because *good* and *evil* are correlated. The struggle for *good* supposes the resistance of *evil*, just as the struggle for freedom supposes the resistance of violence and force. The experience of *evil* enriches *good*, as a result of that creative effort and knowledge which are called into being by contradiction and struggle, as a result of that knowledge which is gained through division and polarization, through submitting to trials. *Good* by itself is powerless to resist *evil*. That is the manifest weakness of legal morality. In its struggle against evil, morality fails to admit grace. A final victory over evil can be achieved only *beyond good and evil*, for it implies a victory not over *evil* but also over *good* in the worldly sense. An integral spirituality differs very much from morality. Morality may want compassion and pity. The law is pitiless, *good* knows no indulgence. But pity and compassion are the kernel of Christian spirituality. The world has no nobler virtues than these. Their action should also include not only those suffering unjustly but also the wicked. A heroic struggle against *evil*, when it is inspired and not merely an expression of legal morality, should not become a merciless persecution of the wicked. Formally interpreted law is merciless not only in its treatment of the wicked, of those who have broken the law, but also of those who suffer, since it is loath to admit the existence of unjust suffering. Within Christian spirituality itself there have been many perversions and legalistic tendencies resulting in a harsh and uncharitable treatment of the suffering on the ground that they were sinners. Is the sinner deserving of compassion and pity? If not, then all men are liable to be treated ruthlessly, without indulgence or compassion. Monastic asceticism frequently took this direction, becoming ill-disposed, merciless and pitiless in its attitude to men. It was held that, since men were sinners, their salvation would be better assured through added suffering. But Christianity is the religion of love, mercy and pity. What is to be done then? There is an apparent clash between the commandment of love and the consciousness of man's sinful nature. All men are guilty; there are no innocent men. Suffering is not merely evil, it is also expiation. But expiation is the peculiar virtue of the suffering of love and willing sacrifice, of a Cross willingly borne. Everything turns on this. It is not only essential to be aware of one's burden, but also to bear the Cross of one's fellow-men, to abstain from condemning them that are no more sinful than I am. Humanism is of Christian origin in so far as it postulated a human and *humane* relationship between men. But humanism differed from Christianity because it tended to interpret man in an increasingly abstract way, as *humanity* rather than as concrete man. Christian spirituality is not fundamentally opposed to humanism; it should be more human and *humane* than humanism; it should acknowledge the absolute validity of each personality and it should be more sensitive to the painful destiny of each man. The paradox of suffering and evil is resolved in the experience of compassion and love. He who loves is aware that a sufferer is not only a sinner, that there is such a thing as unjust suffering. Contemporary psycho-pathology has brought to light in the subconscious human mind deeply rooted instincts of masochism and sadism, man's need to torture himself and others. Dostoievsky and Kierkegaard had already been aware of this fact and had brilliantly illustrated it in their work. Masochistic and sadistic instincts had penetrated into Christian spirituality; they were apparent in monastic asceticism, in Jansenism, in certain forms of Puritanism, in certain other sects, and also in the attitudes which denied man's need for alleviation, for leisure, for imagination, for laughter. The spiritual life has a rhythm; its intensity should seek relief in repose, its suffering in joy, its tears in laughter. Laughter is an independent spiritual problem which has been little investigated. Laughter has a liberating quality which exalts man above his daily worries and oppressive suffering. It must take its place in the spiritual life and help to liberate man from his instincts of masochism and sadism.

IV

The experience of evil and suffering, and the consciousness of them, have instigated a controversy as to the validity of a pessimistic or an optimistic attitude to life. But pure pessimism or optimism is not a spiritual state or attitude to life. The current forms of pessimism and optimism are related to Eudaemonism, and determine their relation to life by the absence or presence of pleasure. But the idea that man is a creature longing for happiness is erroneous, just as the idea of happiness itself is invalid, a mere fiction. Nevertheless pessimism is a profounder attitude to life and shows a greater sensitivity to suffering and evil. Optimism is more superficial and lacks this sensitivity. There is, for example, the optimistic theory of progress which regards every concrete human personality as an instrument of future perfection. Pessimism is a more noble philosophy than optimism, because it is more aware of evil, suffering and sin, of the more profound aspects of life. Christianity is opposed to an absolute hopeless pessimism, but a relative sort of pessimism is in accord with the Christian consciousness. This involves the problem of fate. Does

Christianity admit tragedy? Greek tragedy was founded on the action of fate, on unjust and inexpiable suffering fatally determined. Unjust suffering was eminently tragic; suffering as a consequence of guilt was another matter. Christianity does away with fate, with insoluble destiny. But tragedy survived in the Christian world, although its character was transformed. Christian tragedy is a tragedy of freedom as distinct from a tragedy of fate. This is clearly evident in Dostoievsky's work, which is entirely tragic in character—tragic in the Christian sense. Thus tragedy can be generated by freedom as well as by fate. A final elimination of the tragic element from life would mean the suppression of freedom. The ancient pre-Christian consciousness failed to grasp that fate was related to freedom, that there was such a thing as a fatal freedom. The dark irrational pre-existential freedom becomes transformed into fate. Freedom gives birth to suffering. Spirit is freedom, a freedom fused with the Logos, an illumined freedom assuring the triumph of purpose. Spirituality illuminates freedom, and informs it with purpose. Spirituality is also freedom united with love. Christianity is also aware of unjust or tragic suffering. But it is also aware of unjust suffering as a sacrifice of love. The sacrifice of love is a triumph over the ancient conception of fate, and through it unjust suffering assumes a new significance. But fate continues to be active in the life of the world. In our day, especially, the Marxists claim to have conquered fate. They hold out the promise of a human life so rationalized, so subordinated to collective and social reason, that the irrational, fatal and tragic elements will be completely eradicated from life. In contradistinction to Nietzsche they proclaim their hatred of fate. They represent a rational victory over fate as a triumph of freedom, as a liberation of man from the power of necessity and determination. They are apparently unconscious of the fact that their victory over fate is also a victory over freedom, an extirpation of the freedom of spirit. It would be inadmissible, and even stupid, to deny the possibility of such a rationalization of social life whereby the problem of our daily bread would be solved for all men. A socialized economy on Marxist lines is fully realizable. They are right in this respect. It is hypocritical and shameful to defend an irrational system which condemns people to bitter need and hunger. But this does not help to solve the spiritual problem, it does not prevent man from being confronted with the mystery of death, eternity, love, knowledge and creation. It may even be said that, in face of the increasingly rationalized organization of social life, the tragic element in life, the tragic conflict between the personality and society, between the personality and the cosmos, between the personality and death, between time and eternity, will, on the contrary, become intensified. In fact all the problems of life will become intensified. Spiritual nostalgia, and the terror experienced in face of eternal destiny, will not diminish but increase, and take on more extreme forms. Marxism is not so much a social utopia—it can be socially realized—as a spiritual utopia. The rationalization of social life fails to solve a single spiritual problem, for the spiritual life can be deformed but not rationalized. Attempts to rationalize and regulate the spiritual life merely intensify the tragic conflict between the personality and society. The problem of suffering and evil is not merely a social problem, although it has got a social aspect. It is essentially a spiritual problem. Man will be no happier when his life is better organized; his suffering will merely manifest itself in more subtle and more intense forms. Happiness cannot be organized. While this world persists, beatitude is a mirage. The mystics of all ages have struggled with the eternal foundations of his problem. But mysticism reveals the contradictions inherent in the spiritual life and poses the problem of the new spirituality.

CHAPTER VI

MYSTICISM: ITS CONTRADICTIONS AND ACHIEVEMENTS

I

Asceticism is only an initial stage in the mystical life. It is the stage of purification (κάθαρσις), which is followed by that of illumination (φωτισμός), and, finally, by that of contemplation (θεωρία), the highest achievement of all. Incidentally, many mystics of the intellectualist type insist on the purification of all feelings as well as of sins. The dual significance of mysticism is revealed in mystical writings: it is experience on the one hand, and doctrine (μυεῖν) on the other. Mysticism is a spiritual path leading to the highest achievements. Mystical writings describe this experience and its achievements, its struggle and vision. But there is also a theoretical mysticism which is above all a state of knowledge. Θεωρία is inherent in it from the start; it is the result of inspiration. This is inspired intuitive knowledge. Whereas the first type of mysticism represents the drama enacted between the soul and God, the ascent of the individual soul towards God, the second type is concerned with the cosmic drama—with the drama being enacted even within the Godhead. Thus the human drama is transformed into a cosmic and Divine drama. This does not imply, of course, that theoretical mystics have no personal spiritual experience, because they describe not only the human but also the cosmic and Divine mystery-drama. Mystics like Plotinus and Jacob Boehme had a vast range of spiritual experience. The claims and discoveries of Christian mysticism have always been questioned, debated and subjected to doubt. The pontiffs of Christianity, as of all religions, have invariably regarded mysticism with suspicion as a sphere of inner spiritual freedom hardly amenable to the authority of hierarchical jurisdiction.

Mysticism is opposed to social and objectifying processes; it therefore contradicts historically manifest religion with its social and objectified institutions and hierarchical organization. For that matter, this contradiction holds true not only for mysticism, but also for the spiritual life in general. The criteria of orthodoxy and heresy are inapplicable to mysticism, because they are primarily social in character and are the expression of the sway of a particular religious collective group over the personality. Hence the analogy between mysticism and prophecy. Mystics and prophets are the most free of men, for they refuse to be determined in any way by collective groups, society, or even a religious community. Prophets are distinguished from mystics by the fact that they are the mouthpieces of God and execute the Divine Will to influence the destinies of communities or peoples, whereas mystics are solely concerned with the spiritual world. But, as we shall see hereafter, prophecy is another type of mysticism.

We may resort to conventional terminology and call religion *democratic,* and mysticism *aristocratic*; the first is intended for all men, while the latter is for the few only. Religion appeals to the mass of mankind; it is by nature social, it guides and organizes the life of peoples and communities; it has need of laws, canons, dogma, cultural and moral norms. Hence its primary concern with the lesser forces, with doctrine, with orthodoxy as a social force making for organization and unity. All great religions have given rise to their own particular form of mysticism, which they have first of all attacked as a menace to the social order and then finally sanctified. This was the origin of the canonical form of mysticism which is a contradiction in terms. Although the categories of orthodoxy and heresy are inapplicable to mysticism as well as to the spiritual life, the charge of heresy was frequently levelled against mysticism. These charges were usually inaccurate, because the accusers and the accused were situated on different planes of experience and spoke a different language. Official theology, strong by reason of its social sanction, regarded its dogma as objective truth which must be opposed to the subjective statements of mysticism. This dogma was actually objective in the sense that it was a spiritual objectification. The canonical structure of the Church as a social institution was likewise objective. Actually, mysticism was extraneous to these categories of objective and subjective: it was certainly not subjective, if by that was meant spiritual and contemplative states at the mercy of fantasy. Authentic mysticism is a reality; it is a preoccupation with primal realities, with the existential mystery, whereas orthodox theology treats only of socially consecrated symbols. Mysticism is a *revelation of revelations*, a revelation of the realities behind symbols. The real mystics were realists who could distinguish realities. In this sense realism has nothing in common with objectification. Mysticism is essentially a spiritual as distinct from a psychic state and implies a spiritual penetration of the soul. It is the birth of spiritual man, who apprehends realities in a better and more incisive way than natural or psychic man. *Mysticism is a transcendence of the created world.* This is an essential definition applicable to all forms of mysticism. But the transition from the material to the Divine life is not effected by the natural man, a creature compounded of body and soul, but by the spiritual man in virtue of the spiritual principle inherent in him. In this sense there is a greater affinity between God and man than between man's spiritual and natural natures. Spirituality reveals the divinity inherent in man; but this, in its turn, proves to be profoundly human. This is the fundamental principle governing the relationship between the human and the Divine. But as a state of pure spirituality mysticism may be deformed by man's psychic and corporeal states. This distortion is especially evident in abstract anti-human spirituality, which denies the divinely human nature of mysticism. There exists, therefore, a false spirituality, a state of false spiritual exaltation. There also exists a false mysticism, a false mystical vision and exaltation. Against these states we should always be on our guard.

The eternal conflict between mysticism and theology derives from the fact that they converse in different and untranslatable idioms. Whenever an attempt is made to translate mystical experience into the idiom of theology, it leads to a charge of heresy against the mystics. The idiom of mysticism is paradoxical; it is not intended for ordinary communication or reasoning; it is not a mode of thought governed by the law of identity. The idiom of theology always endeavours to be rational, to avoid contradiction—though in this it is not always successful. It is therefore difficult not to deform mystical thought when rendering it into the idiom of theology and abstract metaphysics. Mystics are constantly being suspected and accused of immanentism—of affirming the immanence of God and of divinity in the soul. True, mysticism, every mysticism, does bridge the transcendental gulf between God and man. In mystical experience the transcendental does become immanent. But it is perfectly obvious that mystical immanence is absolutely different from philosophical immanence, from the immanence of the theory of knowledge and theology. It is a spiritual immanence. Spirituality is the immanence of the Divine in the human, but this does not infer undifferentiated identity. It is paradoxical that while mystical experiment is both a confrontation and an experience of the transcendental, the transcendental is immanent in it; and that the distinction between the transcendental and the immanent is resolved without the Divine being completely absorbed in the human. The Divine is experienced immanently. God is revealed in the primal depths of the soul; everything issues from the depths and from within. Of the spatial symbols, depth and height, mystics prefer the former. But they have no intention of denying the distinction between the human and the Divine. There can be no greater error than to interpret mystical experience in terms of monistic metaphysics. Monism postulates rationalization, a mental process rather than experience. Mystics have also been frequently accused of pantheism, but this only reflects an attempt to translate the paradoxical ineffable experience of mysticism into the rational idiom of theology and metaphysics. Pantheism is first and foremost a theological invention, a weapon of theological debate. In the same way monism is the product of metaphysics, which works in terms of concepts. Thus mystical experience is free from monism or pantheism, from such elaborations of spiritual experience into concepts.

The case of Master Eckhart, one of the greatest of all mystics, is very typical and illustrates the problem of the relation between mysticism and theology. We know that the Catholic Church condemned his mystical writings on the ground of pantheism. This condemnation was generally accepted. But then the Domincan Denifle attempted to prove that Eckhart was an orthodox Thomist in his Latin theological treatises. It would thus appear that Eckhart was an orthodox theologian but an heretical mystic. Without pursuing Eckhart's case any further we are forced to conclude that this contradiction is an example of the incompatibility of the theological and the mystical idioms. The theological translation of Eckhart's mysticism made him appear to be a monist, pantheist and heretic, while in terms of theological concepts he would have been prepared to be a Thomist. It is obvious, therefore, that the concept is fatal to any kind of mystical or spiritual experience. The concept admits the law of identity but not paradox; and its champions are apt to regard mysticism with suspicion or to condemn it. The concept has a social function to perform; it is an instrument for organizing the average man: it operates in terms of the *general* and has no affinity with the particular or the unique. Mysticism is the exact opposite of this. Mystical affirmations such as that God is born in the soul and the soul is born in God, Eternal genesis is peculiar to the depths of the soul, God is more human than man himself, God is within us but we are without, can all dispense with theological concepts.

When Eckhart says, '*Wäre aber ich nicht, so wäre auch Gott nicht*', rational theology can only protest its horrified disapproval.

Similarly, when another great mystic and poet, Angelus Silesius, says 'ich weiss dass ohne mich Gott nicht ein Nu kann leben. War ich zu Nichts, er muss von Not den Geist aufgeben,' theology proves incapable of translating this into its own idiom. The idiom of mysticism is founded on love rather than on precepts. What Angelus Silesius wished to state was that the lover could not exist without the loved. When the loved one died, then the lover also died, since their existence was inseparable from their love. God is He Who loves, He neither can nor would exist without a loved one. Mystics have often affirmed that God and man were reciprocal, Creator and creature. If there were no man, then there would likely be no God. When man was born, then God, too, was born. That is the most profound truth of spiritual experience, a truth revealed in spiritual freedom. This truth can neither be objectified nor expressed in concepts. It does not lend itself to the elaboration of any objective ontology. The mystical truth of man and God united in the depths of the soul contradicts the conception of God as absolute and self-sufficient being. A conception such as this fails to be an expression of the Divine life. It is merely an objective statement reflecting certain aspects of the attempt to organize the religious life in the social sphere. But the affirmations of Angelus Silesius and other mystics are the expression of a paradox revealed in the depths of nonobjectified existence. In the same way the greatest mystic of the Christian East, St. Simon, the New Theologian, spoke in terms which are incomprehensible to rational theology and ontology. Among his sayings are: '*I thank Thee, O God, that Thou, Who reignest over all, art now in very truth and unchangeably one spirit with me.*' '*Suddenly He came and united Himself to me in a manner quite ineffable; He entered into every part of my being, as fire penetrates iron, or light streams through glass.*' '*I rejoice in His love, and in His beauty, and I feel myself overwhelmed with divine happiness and sweetness. I am filled with light and glory; my face shines like that of my Beloved and all my members glow with heavenly light. Then I am lovelier than the loveliest, riche*

*than the richest, stronger than the strongest, greater than the rulers of
the world, more honourable than anything visible, and not only more
honourable than the earth and all that is in it, but also than heaven
itself and everything that it holds.' 'I move my hand and my hand is
wholly Christ's, for God's divinity is united inseparably to me.'* Like
passages may be found in Tauler and in St. John of the Cross. A
theological and metaphysical interpretation only deforms these
truths of mystical experience and introduces pantheistic and monistic associations. Authentic mysticism is not affected by the opposition of transcendental dualism and immanent monism. Mystics
are not content merely to state that the world and man are Divine,
that the creature and the Creator are one in nature. They describe
the abyss separating man from God, the fallen world, the dialogical struggle, the inherent tragedy of the spiritual life. Mystical
experience is a triumph over creatureliness—an achievement
which cannot be adequately described in terms of theological
concepts. Thus theology interprets this as pantheism, whereas it
is nothing of the sort, but something dynamic and inexpressible.
Pantheism is no victory over the creature. As a rational system it
is a form of acosmism, a denial of the reality of the world and of
man; or, again, a form of atheism, a denial of Divine reality, an
affirmation of the divinity of the natural world. Pantheism has
no need of theodicy, since everything in it is *ab initio* Divine.
Aloysius Dempf, the Catholic philosopher, refers in a recent book
of his to Eckhart's work as theo-pantheistic. Theo-pantheism is
a doctrine which maintains God is everything, rather than that
everything is God. In this sense Krause's pantheism was really
theo-pantheism. The need for a new term in this connection
illustrates the difficulty of describing mystical experience in the
idiom of theology and metaphysics. But there has been an attempt
in the history of human thought, in the history of intellectualist
mysticism, to transcend the limits of thought within the confines
of thought itself. No greater testimony to the power of thought
exists than this attempt at self-limitation, this attempt to transcend

its own limits, this *docta ignorantia*, as Nicholas of Cusa defined it. I have in mind, of course, apophatic theosophy.

II

So-called apophatic theology has been upheld by the greatest thinkers, and it is founded on an eternal truth. This eternal truth is the acknowledgment of the Divine mystery inherent in the innermost depths of being. It is an ultimate mystery revealed in existence—a mystery to which no rational concept, no rationalization of being, is applicable. It has no relation to agnosticism and should not be interpreted as such. Spencer believed that the world was founded on the Unknowable, and he was prepared to acknowledge this as the Deity. Positivism claimed to be agnostic. But such a conception implies an absolute and irreconcilable rupture between man and the Unknowable—a separation which is not even experienced as a mystery. Apophatic theology is mystical rather than agnostic. It affirms another truth: the spiritual interpretation of the Divine mystery, the Unknowable, that which positive concepts are unable to express. It further affirms that man is capable of experiencing the Divine, of communing with It, of being one with It. Apophatic theosophy has certain affinities with Hindu philosophy, and for that reason it may appear to be a form of pantheism. It is also true that whatever element of truth there may be in pantheism, it is also applicable to apophatic theosophy but never to cataphic theosophy. It would be more exact to say that the error of pantheism consists in the confusion it produces of apophatic and cataphic elements, in its attempt to interpret apophatic truths in cataphic terms.

Plotinus was the first philosopher of Mediterranean culture who laid great emphasis on the truth of negative theosophy. In him the highest level of Greek wisdom combined with important Oriental spiritual currents. He was thus able to transcend the classic limitations of Greek thought. Plotinus is the greatest of all mystical philosophers, but he is not the greatest of all mystics. Nevertheless Plotinus had definite limitations; and Christian spirituality is immeasurably loftier and more human. But both Christian apophatic theology and Patristic thought owe a great deal to Neo-Platonism. The intellectualist mysticism of pseudo-Dionysius the Areopagite is fundamentally Neo-Platonic in character. And he had a tremendous and determining influence on both Eastern and Western Christian mysticism. He was, all differences aside, the formative influence behind St. Maxim the Confessor, St. Thomas Aquinas and Eckhart. Nicolas of Cusa likewise exercised a considerable influence on the development of apophatic theosophy; he stands on the threshold of two worlds, with his back to ancient and medieval philosophy, pointing the way to modern thought. Plotinus had already affirmed that the concept of being was inapplicable to God, that God was super-Being, that God was Nothing if being was something. In this way, with Plotinus, Greek intellectualism transcends its frontiers and ascends into loftier realms. *Nous* is the intermediary step in the transition from the many to the One. In Nicolas of Cusa positive knowledge stops at *docta ignorantia*. He advances a stage beyond Greek and Scholastic rationalism by his discovery of the principle of contradiction, of antinomy, which is destined to play an important part in the development of future thought. God is the *coincidentia oppositorum*, the co-existence of antitheses—or, in other words, God is inapprehensible through knowledge based on the law of identity. We are here confronted with a remarkable phenomenon in spiritual history. The Divine revelation in the Bible and in the Gospel is that of a God manifest in relation to the world and man, that of the Creator and Providence, that of a cataphic God. This is essentially a religious sphere having nothing in common with philosophy. In mysticism, on the other hand, the soul longs for the non-revealed God, for the God Who has not revealed Himself in history, for the God Who is not even the Creator, for the apophatic God. This fact gives rise to the

most difficult and painful problem of Christian spirituality: How
to reconcile the apophatic and the cataphic knowledge of God in
the spiritual life? This involves the problem of the personality, of
love and of prayer. Pure apophatic mysticism is abstracted and
severed from the plural world, from the concrete man; it is, in
fact, antagonistic to the Gospel commandments. Before considering Christian mysticism, the highest achievements of essential
Christian spirituality, we should do well to examine the destiny
of apophatic theology in the history of German intellectualist
mysticism. This experience has an important bearing not only on
mysticism in general, but also on philosophy in particular.

German mysticism is one of the greatest manifestations of
spiritual history. Eckhart, Tauler, Jacob Boehme, Angelus Silesius,
all draw conclusions from apophatic theology such as were not
to be found in pseudo-Dionysius or medieval mysticism in
general. Eckhart's distinction between *Gottheit* (Godhead) and
Gott (God) proved to be the starting point of this spiritual movement. Indeed this distinction eventually proved to be the basic
intuition of German mysticism and metaphysics. In contradiction
to Greek thought, German philosophy affirms the irrational and
ineffable principle, the mystery of the *Ungrund*, as the primary
basis of existence. In the metaphysical sphere this implies the
supremacy of voluntarism over intellectualism. In theology this
means that *Gott* is a revelation of cataphic knowledge, and
Gottheit is a revelation of apophatic knowledge. *Gottheit* is super-
existence, super-personality, the ineffable depths and genesis of
God. Thus in its essentials theosophy can only be symbolical and
not conceptional. The spiritual experience of mysticism is a
constant demonstration of this. The conception of God expounded
by cataphic theology has always been exoteric in character.
Christian dogma is merely a symbolism of spiritual experience.
The objective processes at work within it cannot be acknow-
ledged as ultimate truth. The mystics do go a step further, but
they can only communicate their experience through symbols

and myths. There is no rational, conceptional way of interpreting Eckhart's *Gottheit* or Boehme's *Ungrund*; their inherent mystery can only be stated in terms of a definitive concept. The conclusions of German mysticism are that neither the Divine Nothing nor the Absolute can be the Creator. The *Gottheit* is not creative; It escapes all worldly analogies, affinities, dynamism. The notion of a correlative Creator and creature is a category deriving from cataphic theology. God-the-Creator comes and goes with the creature. I should state this as follows: God is not Absolute, for the notion of God-the-Creator, God-the-Person, God in relation to the world and man lacks that complete abstraction which is necessary for a definitive concept of the Absolute. The concrete revealed God is correlative to the world and man. He is the biblical God, the revealed God. But the Absolute is a definitive mystery. In consequence two acts are affirmed: Firstly, from the Divine Nothing, from the *Gottheit*, from the *Ungrund*, a God is realized in eternity, a triune God; and secondly, God, the triune God, is the Author of the world. It appears, therefore, that there is in eternity a theogonic process, a Divine genesis. And that is the inner, esoteric life of the Deity. The act of Creation, the relationship between God and man, is the revelation of the Divine drama, of which time and history are an inner content. This conception, which can hardly be called pantheistic, is best of all expressed in Boehme.

Pantheism is essentially of this world; it is a figment of the mind and of the understanding. In relation to this world, we should discard monism in favour of dualism. There is no cataphic way of overcoming dualism; this can be done only apophatically, when objective frontiers are transgressed. Monism and pantheism are both objectified states. The ultimate mystery reveals itself in the subject rather than in the object. That is the secret of all things being absorbed into spirit. German mysticism speaks of *Seelengrund* as the meeting-place with the Divine. But this stratum of the soul is beyond any concept we may have of the world.

Mystical experience transcends the categories of the world, all objectified forms, all our concepts. Mystical experience transcends our conception of the Creator—but not because the Creator and the creature are identified, for that would only situate us on *this side* of the world. Nor should it be maintained that mystical experience is ontological, for it is situated on the *other side* of conceptional being. Our interpretation of being is invariably too naturalistic. Spirit is freedom as distinct from nature. Freedom exercises a primacy over being, which is merely an objectified state, an arrested freedom shaped by mental concepts. By way of contrast, freedom is an apophatic state. Spirituality is impervious to rationalization; it is situated on the *other side* of rational consciousness. But in its deepest manifestations mysticism poses the most difficult of all problems, that of the personality, of personal union, of personal love. Mystical experience is profoundly personal, while at the same time appearing to discard and to dissolve personal existence in the impersonal and super-personal existence. As we shall see, this characteristic constitutes the essential difference between Christian and non-Christian mysticism. The latter is not only abstract, but also incarnate and concrete; it is the mysticism of love.

Here are a few quotations from German mystics which illustrate the difficulty of rationalizing mystical experience. The following is a passage from Tauler, whom Catholics regard as the most orthodox of the German mystics: 'God is a spirit and the soul is a spirit. So the soul is for ever tending and for ever gazing back towards the source of its being. And because of this identity in spirituality the soul tends and stoops back into the first source, into the identity.' There is another even more characteristic passage in Tauler: 'Man uncreated was eternally in God. When man was in God, then man was God in God.' There is also a passage of great interest in Vogel which helps us to distinguish between apophatic and cataphic theosophy: 'But God . . . is either for Himself, absolutely, apart from all creatures, in the mystery of

His unity, or else *respectu creaturarum*, present and active in His manifestation to His creature. God absolute, alone for Himself, apart from all creature, is and remains impersonal, timeless, placeless, inactive, will-less, dispassionate, nor is He Father or Son or Holy Ghost, but He is in eternity beyond time, in every place poised in the dwelling of Himself, working nothing, willing nothing, desiring nothing. But in respect of the creature, *i.e.* with and through the creature, He is personal, active, willing, desiring and suffering. . . . Then also He becomes the Father and He becomes the Son and is Himself the Son, and He becomes the Holy Ghost and is Himself the Holy Ghost, willing, moving, creating all things.' But most interesting of all is, perhaps, Angelus Silesius, the great mystic and poet, who was never condemned by the Catholic Church. Characteristic of him, as of German mysticism in general, is the fact that he can envisage no finality, but pushes his investigations ever further: 'I must pass beyond God into a wilderness.' 'I am as great as God, He is as little as I.' 'When I with God into God am transformed.' 'It is I must be the sun, to give colour with my beams to the colourless sea of the Godhead entire.' 'Man is the greatest miracle; he can, according to his works, be God or Devil.' 'He who seeks God must become God.' Rational theology and metaphysics will tend to debate these mystical statements, to classify them as monism, pantheism or as an identity of God and man. But this tendency only demonstrates the impotence of thought when confronted with the mystery of Divine-human relations as revealed in mystical experience. Mysticism shows above all that the relationship between God and man is a paradox. But the formulas elaborated by theology exclude paradox. Thus mysticism is a spiritual sphere, a spiritual plane, whereas rational theology and metaphysics are only operative on an objectified plane of rationalized and socialized existence.

The mystical gnosis of Jacob Boehme, the greatest Gnostic mystic of all time, presents an almost insurmountable obstacle to rational theology and metaphysics. Boehme differs from Eckhart in that his vision is founded on the Cabala rather than on Neo-Platonism. His gnosis is expressed in myths and symbols rather than in concepts. Boehme is a visionary: he dwells entirely in the spiritual world and his vision is untranslatable in terms of the objective world. He gazes into depths which the objectified world, armed with intellect and concepts, is unable to grasp. Boehme is also penetrated with the biblical spirit. Most important of all is his intuition of the *Ungrund*, about which he says: 'And the cause of the flowing over into being is the wisdom of God; and the cause of the wisdom is the Trinity of the uncausable Godhead; and the cause of the Trinity is the single unfathomable will; and the cause of the will is the nothingness.' And again: 'The uncausable and uncaused is an eternal nothingness, and the cause of an eternal beginning, a craving; for nothingness is a craving for something.'

Is the idiom of theology and metaphysics capable of explaining *Ungrund*? That is a task which only apophatic knowledge can undertake. *Ungrund* is not being, but a more primeval and deeper stratum of being. *Ungrund* is *nothingness* as distinct from *something* in the category of being; it is not οὐϰ ὄν, but μὴ ὄν. But it is not μὴ ὄν in the Greek sense. Boehme goes beyond the limits of Greek thought, of Greek intellectualism and ontology. Like Eckhart's *Gottheit*, Boehme's *Ungrund* goes deeper than God. We should probably be right in thinking of *Ungrund* as the primal pre-existential freedom. For freedom precedes being. Freedom is *not created*. That is the definition I personally should propose. Boehme stands out as the first voluntarist in European thought, although he did not push rationalization as far as the later German voluntarist metaphysicians. The *nothingness* longs to be *something*. The glimmerings of being precede being itself. In the dark void anterior to being freedom is kindled. Boehme's vision discloses fiery and dynamic depths of being, much vaster probably than being itself. There is an affinity between Boehme and Heraclitus;

but Boehme represents, of course, a complete departure from ancient philosophical modes. He introduces the dynamic principle. He attempts to solve the mystery of genesis, of theogonic, cosmogonic and anthropogentic processes. As he sees it, this genesis is not situated within the circumference of the objectified, time-conscious world. *Ungrund* is the undetermined, the groundless, the bottomless; it is situated beyond the world of causality. In philosophical terms it might be described as the impossibility of finding freedom in the objectified or natural world. Freedom reveals itself only in spirit, in the spiritual sphere. Genesis from freedom is a spiritual rather than a natural event. Boehme's vision helped to enrich the thought of Kant, Fichte, Schelling, Hegel and Schopenhauer. But the later German metaphysicians have so rationalized and transformed Boehme's vision that it has assumed a completely non-Christian character out of keeping with Boehme's original intention. His mysticism is essentially Christo-centric. Jacob Boehme and St. Thomas Aquinas represent two divergent types of gnosis. Boehme's grandiose structure is musical and symphonic; that of St. Thomas Aquinas is architectural, like a Gothic cathedral. Boehme's vision is dynamic; St. Thomas Aquinas's is static. The strength and weakness of German meta-physics lies in the fact that it rationalized a musical theme. But by its very nature mysticism is more musical than architectural. How shall we distinguish between Christian and non-Christian metaphysics? That is one of the leading problems evoked by German mysticism.

III

From the manner in which many mystics describe their experiences they might appear to be the exponents of monism, pantheism, anti-personalism, anti-humanism, or of an attitude denying human freedom and love. But as we have already observed, the idiom of mysticism is untranslatable into theological and metaphysical terms. But the problem posed by the mystics still remains unsolved and perturbing. There are two different schools of mystical thought: one deifies the cosmos or man; the other repudiates the cosmos or man. These contrary tendencies can, however, be reconciled. Whenever man and the cosmos become one and identical in a Divine monism, it might also be asserted that man and the cosmos are deified and consequently denied. Monism is invariably a denial of the mystery of Divine humanity, that of dualism which is only completely revealed in Christianity. Christianity is personalistic and manages to reconcile monism and pluralism. The mysticism of love is the only expression of this reconciliation. There is no love without personality, for love is a radiation from one personality to another. Concentration on the personality is for the most part ethical, while concentration of the cosmos is for the most part aesthetic. A sense of ecstatic union with the cosmos is peculiar to a special type of mysticism, just as German National Socialism and Russian Communism are special types of mysticism. But Christian spirituality and mysticism are always distinguished by these three characteristics: personality, freedom, love. Whenever one of these elements is absent, then Christian mysticism suffers thereby. Christian mysticism has, indeed, not infrequently suffered in this manner. This is particularly true of asceticism. Certain non-Christian elements have also penetrated into Christian mysticism. Pantheistic monism is in no sense a heresy against God, but rather and above all a heresy against man, against the personality, against freedom and love. It seems paradoxical, but this tendency can be discerned among those who profess an apparent hostility to pantheism and affirm extreme forms of pantheistic dualism. When it is affirmed that God is everything, that man and the world are nothing, merely pitiful and worthless creatures, mere images of sin, then that is a form of monophysitism and pantheism. Only God is a free agent; His power is manifest everywhere. Human agency is sinful and worthless, since man is lacking in freedom and creative power. Thus, although this system of thought postulates an extreme form of dualism, it tends to develop into an extreme form of monism. It is most remarkable that this spiritual dialectic should be able to pass so easily from one extreme to the other. In the most uncompromising forms of Western asceticism, in those which regard man and the world as entirely sinful, in Calvinism, for example, with its sentiment of Divine power and glory at the expense of man's humiliation, in Barthianism, even, with its belief that God is everything and man nothing, in all these we can observe an almost imperceptible transition from dualism (the transcendental gulf between God and man) to a form, a monism or pantheism, involving not the deification but the humiliation of the world and man. This fact explains how Luther, who believed that human nature was completely corrupted by sin and that reason was a diabolical invention, and who put all his faith in the agency of grace, was able to lay the foundations of the German idealist metaphysics of Fichte, Hegel and Schelling, who, on the contrary, deified reason and regarded man simply as an instrument of the Divine Will. The human reason invariably favours either monism or dualism, and in each case there is a tendency for it to develop into its opposite. Spiritual tendencies are likewise governed by this genuine predilection of human thought, by this inability to co-ordinate the mystery of the One and the many. Thus spirituality itself tends to become either monistic or dualistic. In this way spirituality may either deify the world and man, an obvious form of pantheism, or it may regard man and the world as wholly sinful and lacking in any freedom and creative power, a disguised form of pantheism. In contradistinction to this there is the spirituality based on the union of man and God, on Divine humanity, through which man may be deified without surrendering his human nature to Divine nature. Deification implies a distinction between God and man, a dialogical and dramatic relationship between them. If man were already Divine, or if he were entirely sinful and separated from God by an absolute gulf, then such deification could not take place. This deification or theosis, which is a fundamental feature of Eastern Christian mysticism, is neither a monistic identity with God nor a humiliation of man and the created world. Theosis makes man Divine, while at the same time preserving his human nature. Thus, instead of the human personality being annihilated, it is made in the image of God and the Divine Trinity. The personality can be thus preserved only in and through Christ. The mystery of the personality is intimately related to that of freedom and love. Love and charity can flourish only if there are personal relationships. Monistic identity excludes love as well as freedom. Man is not identical with the cosmos and with God; man is a microcosm and a microtheosis. The human personality can hold a universal content.

The mysticisms of all ages, countries and religions have generic characteristics. By their attributes we can distinguish the types of mystics. They call to each other from different parts of the world. There are greater affinities between the mystics of various religions than between the religions themselves. The depths of spirituality may manifest a greater community than objectified religions. Nevertheless there are different types of mysticism, and the most important distinction is between Christian and non-Christian types. There are two prototypes of non-Christian and pre-Christian mysticism which have persisted throughout Christian history and are still to be found surviving in our day. One of these is the Hindu mysticism of identity, of absolute abstraction from the plural world, of absorption in the *Brahman*. This is an attempt at a mysticism of pure spirituality. It is an acosmic mysticism. *Brahman* and *Atman*, Deity and soul, are identical. The realization of the *Atman* is likewise a realization of the *Brahman*. Sankara, whom P. Otto compares with Eckhart, is a typical representative of this school. God is represented as a super-existential non-being. It would be simpler to call this type of mysticism pantheism. It is a logical apophatic mysticism, one of renunciation and abstraction from any concrete being, from any cosmic and human plurality. It might also be said that the world of becoming, the composite and transitory world, is not authentic being, whereas the escape from it in search of the One is a passage towards authentic being; and that this world is being, but an escape from it is a passage to super-being. The evil and suffering of the plural sensible world are discarded through an act of abnegation and concentration on the abstract non-concrete One. This is an austere and unloving mysticism. The absence of love is explained by the fact that this mysticism is unconscious of the personality; it is concerned with abdicating rather than preserving the personality. As we have already shown, love is the relation of one personality to another. *Ta twam asi* is a term which denotes not love or the union of oneself with another, but the discovery in another person of identical characteristics, thus suppressing personal being. Love, on the other hand, postulates differentiation, the existence of another personality rather than the identity of personalities. The differences between Greek and Hindu philosophies apart, the mysticism of Plotinus answers to this type. It is also a mysticism of the One which is attainable through an abnegation and abstraction of the plural world. In Plotinus there is no mystery of the personality, and therefore no mystery of love. In Platonic and Neo-Platonic philosophy *Eros* aspires to good, supreme happiness, beauty rather than to concrete being or personality. As in Hindu mysticism, the One is super-being and is realized apophatically. Our soul is essentially Divine through spirit, through *nous*. The act of mystical contemplation is identical with the object contemplated, intellection is identical with the intelligible. This is a form of mystical monism, affirming the existence only of the One. Thus the spiritual path leads from complex plurality to simple unity. Being is identical with mind, with *nous*. In Hindu and Platonic mysticism everything is diametrically opposed to the dialogical and dramatic relationship between man and God, between one personality and another, as

revealed in the Bible. Spirituality is interpreted as being opposed
to the personality, and therefore as independent of love, human
freedom, and a relation between the plural and the One. The
mystical way is that of gnosis rather than of Eros. Eros, too, is
explained as a want, as a need of fulfilment rather than as a gift
of abundance. These mystical elements have survived in the
Christian world; they may be traced in Christian Neo-Platonism,
in Eckhart's mysticism, in Quietism. But there exists a non-
Christian mysticism of another type, but equally unfavourable
to the personality and to the notion of a personal relationship
between man and God.

This other type of non-Christian mysticism is cosmic in character. It is an eternal type of mysticism. In communion with the
cosmic elements man feels a sense of liberation from the tyrannical
limitations of individual being, from the pain of personal existence
in the world. This is the Orgiastic type of mysticism. Both
asceticism and Orgiasm can transcend the frontiers of man's
corporeal existence. Orgiasm also implies the mortification of the
flesh. The elemental cosmos—a Divine world—in which man
longs to dissolve his being, appears to be very different from *this
world* of limitations and torturing necessity. Orgiastic cosmic
mysticism unites distinct, limited and determined human existence
with the cosmic soul, the national soul, the terrestrial soul, sexual
elementalism in their most universal non-individualistic manifestations. This mysticism is vitalistic rather than spiritualistic, it
is expressive of soul and body. But this type of mysticism also
aims at overcoming the limitations of consciousness, at breaking
away from the domination of rationalism. It is problematic
whether this path leads man to superconsciousness or to sub-
consciousness. Consciousness is, of course, a pain and a torment;
it is ever an 'unhappy consciousness'. Man can attempt to liberate
himself from it in different ways. But in non-Christian mysticism
all these ways lead to one and the same result—namely, to man's
elimination, to the dissolution of his personality in the elemental

cosmos or in the abstract spirit. Exemption from pain and suffering is obtained through renunciation of personal being, for personality implies the painful process of self-realization. The Dionysian mysteries are a prototype of these cosmic Orgiastic mysteries. They were not of Greek origin and have in them a deep sense of the chthonic subterranean gods. The human personality becomes dissolved in the Dionysian mysteries, in which man surrenders himself to a sort of Divine bestiality. The formalistic genius of Greece transformed these elemental mysteries by mingling the Apollonian with the Dionysian principle. But Dionysian elementalism is eternal, it is the elemental foundation of man and the world, it is inseparable from the tragedy of human passions. The Dionysian cults give expression to a profound nostalgia for union and oneness, a thirst to escape from differentiated existence. In them man communes with the One and achieves union in the very depths of cosmic plurality itself. Man achieves the same result in Neo-Platonism by renouncing cosmic plurality through the abstract spirit. In this case man transcends himself through asceticism. But this transcendence of self also appears as an end of self, as personal being. The Dionysian element is still active in the Christian world. Its manifestations are particularly noticeable at the peak of civilization, when human existence appears to be completely formulated and when every irrational element appears to have been suppressed. Thus Nietzsche rediscovers Dionysus. Polaristic forces are always active in the world. Whenever a culture becomes too formalistic, whenever a civilization becomes too rationalistic, then there ensues a reaction of the irrational forces, of the Dionysian elements. Man longs to commune with the *natural* and the *irrational*. This may take the form, as in Klages, of the *soul's* reaction against *spirit*. Writers like Rozanov and D. H. Lawrence are, indeed, characteristic of the cosmic mysticism of the last generation. But the same holds true of all these mystical trends; communion with the cosmic elementalism of sexuality is the end of personal being, of a personal relationship between man and God, between man and man. And nothing poses the problem of Christian spirituality in a more acute form.

Is an element of Quietism an inseparable part of mysticism? That is a fundamental problem of the new spirituality. The ramifications of Quietism go much farther than the seventeenth-century French mystical currents, than the influence of Madame Guyon and Fénélon. Quietistic elements can be detected in most mystical movements. Catholics regard Luther as a quietiest in so far as he denies human freedom in relation to Divine grace. The essence of the quietistic element in mysticism is a belief in absolute human passivity in relation to God and Divine grace. It is assumed that human nature in a state of absolute passivity is interpenetrated by Divine nature, which alone is active. Divine agency requires a complete inaction on the part of human nature. But this is another form of monophysitism and monism. This is also true of Eastern asceticism, according to which there is no interaction between God and man, but only Divine agency in the face of man's mystical passivity. Madame Guyon, Molina and others went so far as to affirm that mystics could not sin and therefore had no need of repentance. French thinkers, who are hostile to both Quietism and Rousseau, attempt to trace the origin of Rousseau's theory of man's natural goodness and happiness to Quietism in general and Fénélon in particular. The goodness of human nature is the result of Divine agency on man while his own nature, always prone to evil, is in a state of passivity. Tolstoy's doctrine of non-resistance to evil falls into the same category. All evil is the result of man's active resistance and violence; but evil will disappear when man is non-aggressive and passive, for then God Himself, Divine nature, will be operative. In any case this doctrine repudiates the agency of two natures and is therefore monophysitical. A spirituality of this kind denies the element of freedom in man, his free creative activity. These are considered to be the exclusive property of the Godhead. It would be incorrect to say that Fénélon's unselfish love for God is uniquely quietist, for it can be justified on other grounds. But Quietism is to be found also in the Buddhist Nirvana and in Stoic apathy as well as in the Neo-Platonic mysticism of the One and its emanations, in Syrian asceticism with its repudiation of sinful human nature, in Eckhart with his monistic mysticism of identity for which the mere fact of human existence is a fall, and in Karl Barth, who envisages the realization of Christianity in a purely eschatological perspective. But in face of quietist spirituality we must reaffirm the notion of Divine humanity, of man's creative activity. Of all relations the most mysterious and the most difficult to realize in life is that between freedom and Divine grace, between the human soul and Divine or Holy Spirit. This relation defies both monistic and dualistic interpretation; it is situated outside our category of thinking. Both mystical monism and Quietism fail to grasp this relation. Man's inspiration comes from God and from freedom, from Divine grace as a gift from the Deity, from the primordial, ineffable non-determined human freedom. This then is the great mystery of the spiritual life, which no monistic system is able to explain without doing violence to it. The spiritual life is both dualistic and monistic; it is a confrontation, a dialogue, an interaction, an agency of one upon another; it is, in short, divinely human. In the depths of spirit there is a genesis not only of God in man, but also of man in God; there is speech—not only of God, but also of man replying to Him. There is man's nostalgia for God; and there is also God's nostalgia for man, God's need of man.

IV

The essential difference between the Christian East and the Christian West is revealed in their different types of spirituality. Christian mysticism has a common origin, but there are peculiar features distinguishing Eastern mysticism from Western mysticism. It would be an error to say that one or the other type was definitely superior. It is important, however, to grasp this dissimilarity, which was already apparent when the Greek Fathers were confronted with St. Augustine. The Catholic West may distinguish certain pantheistic and Gnostic tendencies in the East. The Orthodox East claims this to be an ontological element and, in its turn, accuses the West of being too psychological and anthropological. The Christian mystics of the East are, of course, permeated to a far greater extent by Neo-Platonism than the Christian mystics of the West. For them everything descends from on high. There is no gulf between the Creator and the creature such as exists in the Catholic and Protestant West. Theosis bridges this gulf. The sensible world is symbolical of the spiritual world (St. Maxim the Confessor). Through the Divine image the creature participates in the Divine qualities. Man's ideal nature is revealed in Christ. Human nature is consubstantial with the human nature of Christ. In the East the human element is permeated by the Divine, while in the West the human element ascends towards the Divine. The Divine agency makes man one with God. The East interprets union with God physically or ontologically. The purpose of redemption is treated physico-ontologically rather than morally and legally. Through Christ the whole of the human race participates in the Divine. This divinization is achieved through the mind understood integrally and ontologically. St. John of the Ladder says: '*The mind must seek to become pure.*' This purity or wholeness of mind is achieved by keeping the conscience within the heart. This is a form of concentration and temperance. The mind is absorbed into the heart. In this way Eastern Christian mysticism has already departed from Neo-Platonism and Greek intellectualism. St. Augustine, on the other hand, makes a synthesis of neo-Platonic intellectualist mysticism and Gospel ethical commandments. In the East the process of transforming neo-Platonic intellectualism assumed other forms. Nature is made Divine by the real presence of the

Deity. Eastern Christian mysticism is not interested in the life
on this earth of Jesus Christ or in the idea of imitating His passions.
The idea of stigmata is likewise foreign to it. It is far less anthro-
pogonic than Western Christian mysticism; it is far less concerned
with man's complex life on earth, with his struggle in life. The
object of contemplation is not humanity, but the divinity of
Jesus Christ. As a result, the East has almost none of those con-
fessions, diaries, autobiographies, accounts of the spiritual life of
saints and mystics which are so common in the West. St. Augustine's idea that a knowledge of God is attainable through a knowledge of the human soul is equally foreign to the East. Thus
Eastern mysticism is less dialogical and less dramatic than Western
mysticism. In spite of its strong intellectualism Western Christian
mysticism is far more emotional than its Eastern prototype.
German mysticism is, however, an exception, and it is in many
ways nearer to Eastern mysticism. St. Bernard is an example of a
purely emotional mysticism that has no equivalent in the East.
Orthodox theology is often injust in the exaggerated accusations
of erotism which it levels against the West. They are founded
upon the fact that Catholic mysticism is more dramatic, for it
portrays man's longing for a God Who is also an object of love.
For Eastern mysticism God is in no sense an object of passionate
aspiration, but is the love permeating man. In Eastern mysticism
there is no experience such as that of the ' *dark night*' of sensibility
and reason in St. John of the Cross, for it has no great interest in
human life; its struggle in the world and its spiritual life are
determined wholly from on high. But there is, instead, an austere
asceticism of another kind. Mysticism is the path of illumination.
In fourteenth-century Byzantine mysticism the ideal was a complete peace of soul, stillness, a domination of the Eros by gnosis.
The love of the heart is restless. The struggle with evil is one
against man's desire for things; it is the achievement of impartiality. Hence it is difficult for an Eastern mystic to be a poet, as
were St. John of the Cross and St. Francis of Assisi. In St. Maxim

x

the Confessor love is metaphysical and intellectual rather than ethical and emotional. The spiritual state is Θεωρια. In St. Isaac the Syrian love is the birth of gnosis. St. Simon the New Theologian is more complex. He approaches nearest of all to St. John of the Cross. But Catholics, in their turn, detect an erotic element in him. St. Simon the New Theologian was a poet. In him there is a dialogue between the human soul and Christ. But for all his peculiarities he remains representative of Eastern mysticism, blending in himself the intellectualist mysticism of gnosis with the affective mysticism of *Eros*. But such phenomena as *stigmata* are unacceptable to Eastern thought. Nor do disease and physical suffering play such an important part as they do in Catholic mysticism. The Orthodox East, and especially Russia, loves St. Francis as the saint who most nearly fulfilled the Gospel image of Christ. But there were traits of Western chivalry in St. Francis which are not to be found in St. Seraphim of Sarov, a typical representative of Eastern mysticism with its ideal of illumination and the divinization of the creature. Eastern mysticism is predominantly that of resurrection whereas Western mysticism is mainly that of crucifixion.

Popular mysticism was chiefly liturgical and sacramental. It expressed the spiritual life of the people. The liturgical poverty and austerity of Protestantism have helped to weaken its hold on the popular masses. Both Orthodoxy and Catholicism have produced their own types of spirituality corresponding with particular liturgical practices. Thus in popular Catholicism we have the *petites dévotions* and particular cults such as the Heart of Jesus, and so on. In Orthodoxy there is a greater homogeneity. Liturgical mysticism raises the problem of the relation between mysticism and magic. In popular liturgy there is an important element of magic which was abused for the purpose of influencing the masses. Protestantism is very right to condemn magic, but at the same time it commits the error of almost identifying mystery with magic. The principles of mysticism and magic are not only different, but diametrically opposed. Mysticism is a spiritual force while magic is a natural force; mysticism is freedom, magic is power. Mysticism is communion with God, magic is communion with cosmic forces generating power. Magic was the first technical means at man's disposal in his struggle against inimical forces, against spirits and demons; it was a technical source of power over the gods themselves. Occultism is related to magic. Magic is never spiritual, although magical elements find their way into the spiritual life. Mysticism is, however, always spiritual. Its distinguishing quality is freedom of spirit—a quality denied to magic, which remains, indeed, the servant of causality and determination. The bondage of the world is a magical phenomenon. But the task of spirit is to break this spell, to end this bondage. This is, indeed, the foremost problem of the spiritual life. In their own way contemporary psychology and psycho-pathology provide evidence of the part played by magic in human individual and collective life. The psycho-analytical method claims to free the consciousness from illusions and pathological traumas, but it is not a spiritual method. Spirituality cannot be merely psycho-analysis; it must necessarily be psycho-synthesis. Spiritual development makes for a synthesis of man's spiritual and corporal life; it also arrests the analytical disruption and disintegration of the whole personality. In magic is concealed a will to bind the world; in mysticism there is a will to liberate the world.

Although prophetism is opposed to any kind of magic, it is not opposed to mysticism. There is a special type of prophetic mysticism. In his work *Das Gebet* Heiler distinguishes between mysticism and prophetism, between mysticism and prophetic religion. Prophetic religion is the religion of a revealed personal God. Mystical religion is the religion of illumination and salvation. This definition calls for criticism, for mysticism rises above the idea of salvation and does not at all coincide with sacramentalism. But Heiler's distinction is nevertheless real. According to him mysticism is passive, quietist and contemplative, whereas prophetism is active, militant and ethical. Love is the peculiar feature of mysticism, faith that of prophetism. Mysticism is extra-historical, prophetism is historical. In mysticism God is neither the Creator nor is He revealed; in prophetism God is the Creator and He is revealed. Prophetic religion is social, mystical religion is not social. Prophetism is masculine, mysticism is more feminine. Heiler will not admit prophetic mysticism as a type distinct from both Gnostic and liturgical mysticism. I personally am inclined to affirm the existence of a particular type of prophetic mysticism. ' The prophet is a man inspired by the Divine Spirit and conversing with God, a man free from the power of the world, of nature and society, a man beholding clearly the paths of freedom as well as those of necessity. The prophet dwells in his own spiritual world; and therefrom he judges the world around him. The prophetic spiritual experience is the contrary of apathy, impartiality, or indifference to the destinies of the world and of history. The Platonist Malebranche made this typical statement of abstract spirituality: '*N'aime aucune création; Dieu n'a fait ton cœur que pour lui.*' These words do not become a prophet, nor would he heed them; his heart is stricken by human destiny, by the destiny of peoples, by the destinies unfolded in world history. That is his vocation; and that is also why he spurns Quietism. Prophetism is revolutionary. It is revolutionary in the sense in which the Bible and the Gospel are revolutionary, while Neo-Platonism, Syrian asceticism and ritual piety are not revolutionary. Devotion is a spiritual act; but when liturgical and solitary devotion is regarded as the only way of salvation from falsehood and suffering, then there is undoubtedly a ritualistic perversion and restriction of spirituality.

Heiler's definition has a biblical and Protestant character. For him Luther and Protestantism are prophetic. Protestantism is a religion of Word and faith. Man obeys God without beholding Him or the Divine world. This conception is clearly expressed in Karl Barth. Man is the *Hörer.* The mystical contemplation of God is a temptation and an illusion. But Protestantism is not only prophetic, it has also produced Pietism (Spener, Peterson, Franck). But the prophetic fire of early Protestantism soon began to die. Its place was taken by a bureaucratic and mechanical organization of the spiritual life in the Protestant Churches. No Church can, of course, escape this process of degeneration. Pietism was the reaction against this despiritualization, a return to inner spirituality—to the *Innerlichkeit*. There is a strong quietist element in Pietism, a tendency to escape from the suffering and the burdens of the world into a comfortable inner world. German Pietism (1670–1720) was on the whole a lower middle-class movement. Its vision was very narrow and alien to the heroic prophetic spirit. But this was only natural, a universally observable phenomenon in fact. First of all the prophetic creative fire is kindled, then the fire dwindles; a bureaucratic organization is set up to govern the spiritual life of the Church; then comes a reaction, a return to an inner life, but that inner life becomes very narrow and the result is bourgeois spirituality. And then the rekindling of a religious prophetism becomes really imperative. Prophetism and mysticism are the two principles that can revive again the still fires of the spiritual life. But the new spirituality should include both these principles. There is a note of eternal truth in the voice of the prophet when he condemns a petrified spirituality and its ritualistic forms.

CHAPTER VII

THE NEW SPIRITUALITY
THE REALIZATION OF SPIRIT

I

All I have previously said in this book has been by way of preparing the revelation of a new spirituality. We should think of spirit and the spiritual life *historically*, but not as historians apt only to obscure the workings of spirit in the course of their objective investigations. History for me is an existential mystery, a destiny. An historical interpretation of spirit postulates a non-hermetic time: a time contained within eternity and interpenetrated by it. Time is a fundamental form of the objectification of human existence. But temporal history has meaning only in the light of the ages and periods of the spiritual kingdom concealed behind its façade. Spirit has an historical existence; hence there are crises of spirit, there is a *kairos* in history, and hence we can also speak of a new spirituality. There is only one eternal spirituality, triumphing over and transcending time; but since spirit is also historical, since it is a realization of destiny, the eternal spirituality can also be a new spirituality. The problem of a new spirituality is posed by the world crisis of spirit, by the prevalent attitudes of hostility to and denial of spirit. This negation of spirit and spirituality is merely another aspect of the decay of an old spirituality and of the abuse to which that spirituality had been put in the interests of selfish human ends. It is not true, therefore, to say that spirituality is lacking in those who deny or vehemently decry spirit. As often as not they are victims of delusion, men who have been unable to endure any longer the trials associated with the decay and the perversion of spirit. Nevertheless in the world to-day there is not only a crisis of spirit reflected to some extent in anti-spiritual activities, but there is also an actual process of weakening and diminishing spirituality. These latter tendencies are the result of an increasing objectification of human existence. But even before this apparent collapse of spirituality it was evident that spirituality had already become so objectified and so conventional as to lose all its inner force. The aim of the new spirituality should be to restore this inner force to authentic existence.

Is objectification a spiritual conquest of the world, a permeation of the world by spirit? And is a restored inwardness merely an escape from the world? These are fundamental and very difficult questions. We are here confronted with the paradox of spirit. Objectification is the way in which spirit adapts itself and conforms to the world; it is a failure of spiritual creativeness, a subjection of the personal element to the general, of the human element to the non-human, of inspiration to law. But in the sphere of objectified existence spirituality may take the form of a denial of and an escape from the world, of an asceticism at once anti-human and hostile to the world. The revival of inwardness may prove to be a revolutionary act in relation to the objectified world; it may prove to be a revolt against determinism or, in other words, a spiritual permeation of the world in order to inspire and transfigure it. The objectification of spirit, far from being an inspiration of the world, an act of indulgence, and a manifestation of the Christian spirit of love and charity, has implied the tyranny of the world and the triumph of everyday social life. Asceticism as a flight from the world has often been subservient to the world and its ways, and has been accompanied by the consecration of the powers ruling the world. But asceticism in the world, the exercise of love and charity, may really change, may even transfigure the world. In the light of the new spirituality, spirit will conquer and transform the world instead of denying it and humbly abandoning it to its fate; and instead of objectifying itself in necessity, it will rule the world through the inner and always deeply personal life; and dispelling the phantasmagoria of the general, it will bring about a personalistic revolution. This is a sign that spirituality seeks above all the Kingdom of God, and not the objectified kingdom of this world. And at this stage we are confronted with the paradoxical relation between personal and social salvation.

The tendency to regard the spiritual life as a way of salvation, and Christianity as a religion of personal salvation, has led to spirituality being narrowed, diminished and weakened. The attitude of men to social and historical life was objectified, and they realized spirituality only in a symbolical way. The objectified forms of social and historical life, its conventional symbolism, its consecration of relative and transitory phenomena, all affected the spiritual life, subjecting it to social and restricting influences. Spirit became the slave of its own objectifying processes. The external manifestations of spirit came to be regarded as the expression of its inner and sacred force. Thus the interpretation of the spiritual life exclusively in terms of personal salvation led to the suppression and social enslavement of spirituality. The longing above all for the Kingdom of God, for the truth revealed in it, is not merely a longing for personal but also for social salvation. The symbolism of socially sacred phenomena, such as monarchy, national government, property, tradition, is no road to salvation. Salvation comes only through realizing or establishing truth in human relationships, in those of the Ego and Thou, the Ego and We, through realizing community or the brotherhood of man. As a result, personal spirituality becomes more free and comprehensive. A purer spirituality is a sign of greater concreteness rather than of greater abstraction. Personal salvation comes to those who seek universal salvation or the Kingdom of God. The idea of personal salvation is a transcendental egoism, a projection of egoism into the eternal life. In this way man's relationship with God becomes a selfish one, an obstacle to the achievement of pure spirituality. This relationship is abstracted from the context of human relationships, the commandment of

Christ and of the Gospel is violated, and the whole Divine humanity of Christianity is sundered. Individual, isolated salvation is an impossibility. Salvation can only be achieved with the help of one's fellow-men, other people and the world. Each man should accept the pain and torment of the world and of other men, and he should share their destiny. Every man is answerable for his fellow. How can I be saved if other men and the world are doomed to perish? Moreover, the very idea of salvation is an egocentric expression of the longing for a full and complete existence, for life in the Kingdom of God. The utilitarian aspect of salvation only deforms the spiritual life. It has led to a denial of human creativeness as a manifestation of spirituality. Thus the whole of man's creative life would appear to have been either condemned or relegated to the extra-spiritual, secular sphere. This is the source of the dualism disrupting man. Humanity appears to live on two different planes executing two different rhythms. There is a rigid division between the sacred and the profane spirituality; the first is hailed as an embodiment of truth while the latter is barely tolerated. Sacred spirituality is essential to salvation, profane spirituality can even become an obstacle to salvation. Thus it is better to be less spiritual than only profanely spiritual. The world appears abandoned to its own problems and torments, it appears doomed to perish. Free and isolated from the plagues of the world, sacred spirituality points the way to salvation.

The torturing problem of predestination, of the chosen few, is intimately related to the conception we have just outlined. The new spirituality repudiates the notion of the elect. It believes that each man must shoulder the destiny of the world and of mankind; that he must aim at freedom and achieve it as his spirituality develops; but this freedom must not be man's abstraction from the world or his refusal to share in the problems and torments of the world for the sake of his own personal salvation. On the contrary, man must feel himself independent of and spiritually antagonistic to the world in order that he may penetrate into the human world, sunk in nostalgia and in a presentiment of doom. The discovery that spirituality is also a social manifestation helps to liberate it for personal creativeness. Spirtuality is always deeply personal, whereas its intention is social and even cosmic. The social restrictions hampering spirituality give it a bias towards personal salvation. Its liberation from social influences helps to direct it towards creative action in the social and cosmic spheres. An emancipated spirituality is preoccupied with universal salvation. Christianity should at once be free of the world, revolutionary in its attitude towards it, and also full of love for it. Hence there are two schools of asceticism: that of flight from the world and that of action in the world. The new spirituality will favour only the second type of aceticism. Some of the elements of this new spirituality are already to be found in the Christian spirituality of the Renaissance, in Nicolas of Cusa. Pico della Mirandola, Paracelsus, Erasmus and St. Thomas More. But the further development of humanism did not realize these possibilities. The spirituality based exclusively on personal salvation can no longer be justified, because the personal and the social act have become indistinguishable. Every personal human act has social consequences and all social acts are determined by personal acts. Personal monastic asceticism frequently sets an evil social example by tolerating social evils and injustice, by sanctifying the existing order of things, and by insisting on passive obedience in the face of falsehood and injustice. A spirituality endeavouring to transfigure and conquer the world postulates personal spiritual activity, a spiritual independence of worldly determination. All the old Christian precepts of spiritual life insisted that man must shoulder the burden of the Cross. But there was a tendency to forget that the cross had a universal significance and application. The Crucifixion awaits not only the individual man but also society as a whole, a State or a civilization. In this light only can we understand the sporadic nature of historical and social pro-

cesses, the mistake of attempting to interpret them exclusively
from an organic standpoint. In its application to social life the
Cross does not imply an acceptance of social conditions, but rather
an acceptance of the idea of inevitable catastrophe, revolution and
radical social changes. It is a profound error to regard the Cross
in a conservative light.

It is because man is interested in social transfiguration, as well
as in his personal salvation, that his deeply personal vocation is
revealed in the spiritual life. This vocation is absent when the
spiritual life is entirely absorbed in personal salvation. Vocation
always involves creativeness; and creativeness is always concerned
with the world, with other men, with society, with history. The
notion of obedience has had a fateful influence on the history of
Christian spirituality. Obedience is pseudo-spirituality. It inevitably involves obedience to evil and a slave mentality. In the name
of obedience Christians have suffered evils so long, that others—
non-Christians—have at last been forced to rebel against them
and to subdue them, but at the price of attacking Christianity
itself. Obedience was an instrument of government which more
than any other exhausted Christian spirituality. Traditional forms
of obedience were inculcated by invoking the punishments of
eternal damnation and infernal torture. Insistence on obedience
led Christianity to evolve the notion of personal salvation and
to become an expression of transcendental egoism. Obedience
was a means by which Christians might hope to procure exemption from fulfilling Christ's commandment. If man were obedient
he might be pardoned for not realizing these commandments in
this life. Metaphysically this implied a complete renunciation of
the human will, even when manifest in love for one's fellow-
men, in pity and charity towards all creatures. Thus war was de-
clared against human nature rather than against the evils of the
world. Furthermore, war against evil became impossible when
the human element was suppressed. Man was abandoned in a
state of terror and servility and, instead of alleviating him, spirit-

uality only made his position worse, justifying his abasement and imputing to it a transcendental character. Indeed this proved to be the origin of reactionary Christianity—an obscurantist force hostile to human freedom and creativeness, to the illumination and transfiguration of the world and human life. But there is a creative spirituality which can liberate man from his servility, terror and abasement, from his egoism and the burden of his blindness. In the creative urge, in the impulse towards liberation, there is a manifest working of grace. The problem of salvation and creativeness, of the part played by creativeness in the spiritual life, is a fundamental one involving the whole future of spirituality in the world and the very possibility of a new spirituality. Christian love itself should be conceived as a great revelation of creativeness in life, as a creation of new life. Feuerbach's atheism was a dialectical moment in the purification and the development of the Christian consciousness. It was Feuerbach who affirmed that knowledge of being is attained through love, that the knowing man is the loving man, that love is being. Being is not that which is apprehended, but that which is loved. Feuerbach has certain affinities with existential philosophy, for he seeks to discover the Thou rather than the object. He affirmed the unity of one man and another, that of the Ego and Thou. For him the knowing man was the whole man apprehending through his reason, heart and love. Feuerbach's atheism is a standing reproach to the old Christian consciousness, to theological doctrines which insisted on obedience rather than on Christian love; for it was the duty of Christians to have affirmed the truths discovered by Feuerbach. Love is creativeness, knowledge is creativeness, the transfiguration of nature is creativeness, freedom is creativeness. Obedience, on the other hand, was a means of stifling creativeness and inspiration, an instrument of man's humiliation.

II

It is inexact to say that man is spirit; but it can be said that he has spirit. The distinction between *being* and *having* is only completely resolved in God. Man is not what he has. He has reason, but he is not reason; he has love, but he is not love; he has quality, but he is not the essential quality; he has an idea, but he is not the idea. The problem of realizing the personality consists in being what one has, in being taken for what one *is* rather than for what one *has*. *To be* is a reality, a realization; *to have* is but a symbol of possession. Socialism might be defined as a passage in the social life from symbols to realities, from a state of *having* something (*property*) to a state of *being* something. The aim of Socialism is to free man from accumulation and saving—from the fictions and symbols of power which have no human reality and only mutilate life. That is the Socialist ideal; but in practice, as in Russian Communism for example, Socialism assumes conventional forms. Man has spirit, but he must also become spirit, an incarnate spirit. And man is capable of this when he is in spirit, when he is inspired. What does it mean to *have* and *to be* spirit? *To be* definitively spirit is theosis or participation in the Divine life. Spirit is from God. And when man *has* spirit, when he is in spirit, then spirit enters into him and inspires him. Hence there is an indissoluble tie between spirit and inspiration or the creative spirit. The problem of creativeness is the fundamental problem of the new spirituality. But in essence spirituality is always creativeness, since freedom and activity are the attributes of spirit. In creativeness there are two elements: that of grace, of inspiration coming to man from on high, of genius and talent possessed by man; and that of freedom, having no external cause and determination, but forming the new elements in the creative act. Creativeness implies interaction not only between man and the world, but also between man and God. It would appear as if, through creativeness, man were presenting the world with his dialogue with God. There are always two actors, there is always a confrontation. Monism is in all its manifestations a false and sterile doctrine. Creativeness cannot be deduced from being interpreted as a whole. It might be said that the *Creator* had spirit and that the *created* had existence. Eckhart was aware of this distinction in spite of his monistic tendency. Spirit is always the creator. Every creative change in the world is the result of the intervention of spirit in being—that is, of freedom and grace. If the union of the soul with God does not imply an identity in nature and substance, that is because spirit is neither nature nor substance. We might state this in a subtler way: spirit, which is neither nature nor substance, is not even being, since freedom is not being. A system of thought based on eternal being as the origin of all determination is inevitably a static system incapable of comprehending freedom, change, novelty, creativeness and even evil. But opposed to this system there is another which affirms the existence of independent freedom as well as of determined being. This involves a different conception of spirit and of the spiritual life. It becomes impossible to conceive of the spiritual life otherwise than as a creative life. The denial in the past of the creative function of spirituality can only signify one thing, that spirituality was included in a system of determined and hermetic being. Spirit was placed in a dilemma: it might ally itself with the forces of light or with the forces of darkness. And these forces—the Divine and the satanic—were represented as finite consolidated systems of being. But actually the Divine life may be interpreted dynamically as a conflict, as a dramatic destiny. Then spirituality appears in a new light. That is the problem of contemplation and action.

In the past mysticism was always conceived as contemplation. Blissful contemplation was described as the ultimate stage of mystical spiritual experience. Contemplation was a state of mystical passivity, of exceptional receptivity. The contemplator is a seer rather than an actor in the drama. Ascetic purification was the only activity involved in mystical contemplation. But contemplation was not thought to imply a possible change in the contemplator. Thus contemplation postulates an eternal, hermetic and finite circle of being immune from external intervention and complete in itself. But the problem is to what extent contemplated being is a concept, the result of conscious elaboration. In this case thought and consciousness are active, but the solid results of this activity are to make man a passive contemplator. Only when he frees himself from the objectification of concepts, from the notion of static being, does man begin to understand the essentially active and creative nature of the relation between man and being, between man and God; and that the essence of spirituality as an impulse of freedom consists precisely in this. There is undoubtedly an element of contemplation in the spiritual life, but it is only a moment, a form of creativeness. This contemplation helps to transform contemplated being. Man responds creatively to the Divine call by effecting a change not only in human life, but also in the Divine life itself. Thus is enacted the Divine-human drama. Contemplation and activity should not be considered as antithetical principles. In the active spirit there are moments of contemplation, when, for example, we transcend the temporal world, but it is essential to grasp the dynamic nature of this act. This problem is of particular importance in the light of present-day actualism. The product of a technical civilization, this actualism is essentially a reflection of human passivity rather than of human activity. Man passively obeys the accelerated tempo of time, which exacts a maximum of activity from him, as a function of a technical process rather than as an integral personality. This activity only disrupts the human personality and the integral human image. It is accompanied by complete spiritual passivity and spiritual death. In contradistinction contemplation is a sign of spiritual activity, of man's resistance to the inroads of technical actualism. In this connection we must consider the problem of time and eternity, man's ability to experience the instant detached from the torrent of time. As Kierkegaard has said, instants should be atoms of eternity rather than atoms of time. Creative activism is invariably a sign that objectification, that ruler of man's entire life, has been transcended. But present-day technical actualism is, on the contrary, a sign of man's final submission to objectifying processes and of the loss of his spirit and freedom. As a result, spirit is interpreted as an epiphenomenon, as a product of material technical processes. Thus spirit appears to be situated either in the passive contemplation of the past, where its creative nature is denied, or in the actualism of present-day technical civilization which altogether denies spirit and spirituality. We are therefore confronted with the problem of a new creative spirituality which shall overcome both the passive contemplation of the past and the passive actualism of the present. Like the spirituality of the past this creative spirituality should be concerned with eternity, but it should also actualize itself in time in order to transform the world. Thus I understand by creative spiritual activity not only the creation of cultural products which are always symbolical, but also a real transformation of the world and of human relationships—in other words, the creation of a new life, of a new being. This implies the triumph of prophetism over ritualism in the spiritual life. It also implies that the need for truth and justice should predominate over the experience of passive ecstasies. And this brings us to the problem of spirituality in relation to social truth.

III

A rigid dualism of spiritual and social life is completely erroneous. For the social life, taken as a whole to include human relationships, and economics, regarded for the most part as a material phenomenon, are both products of spirit. Spirit alone is active, matter is passive. The economic system is the result of man's struggle against nature and is, therefore, the result of human

L

spiritual activity. The social life is wholly dependent on men's spiritual state. Diverse forms of spirituality determine the character of human labour and man's attitude to the economic system. A great deal of light has been thrown on this problem by the work of Max Weber, Troeltsch, Sombart and De Man. But there is another side to the problem: men's spiritual life is influenced by their social life; social forms leave their imprint on spiritual forms, even on man's conception of God and on his interpretation of dogmas. Spiritual forms are intimately related to the forms of human association, to the forms of human relationships. Christianity may change, not as a result of any new revelation, but simply as a result of a change in the human environment receiving the revelation. Christianity may be adopted by a humanized or a bestial environment. And a particular environment depends on the nature of its human relationships. In an environment in which men behave like wild beasts, in which men oppress and exploit their fellow-men, men's spiritual life and theosophy will be affected thereby. Human knowledge depends on the degree of community between men, on the forms of their association, and on the character of human labour. In this connection Marx has contributed a great deal of truth, but he vitiated it by his fundamental misconception of spirit. In his just reaction against abstract idealism Marx attempted at first to apply spirit in the social sphere, but he later repudiated spirit altogether. Marx was right in his contention that the historical process was essentially a struggle on the part of man, as a social being, against the elementary forces of nature. For some reason, however, Marx decided that this was a materialistic interpretation of history, whereas actually this struggle, like every other form of human activity, was a spiritual struggle whose results were dictated by man's spiritual state. When Marx asserted that spirit and spirituality were determined by economics, there is only one possible interpretation of this—namely, that spirit must be liberated from the tyranny of economics, from slavery and falsehood. His indictment is just; but in affirming that spirit and spirituality are born of economics he propounds an absurdity which Marxists have failed so far to explain logically. Spirit can never be an epiphenomenon; it is primary, it is freedom. Only a limited or deformed spirit and spirituality can be an epiphenomenon. Class interests breed only falsehood, never truth. We can define the relation between spirituality and social life thus: when spirituality is dependent on the social environment, it is perverted and deformed, it is a form of slavery and symbolical falsehood; truth, justice and freedom, on the other hand, are the result of spiritual activity in the social environment and in man's relationships. If spirit is passive in relation to the social life, if spirituality is completely divorced from the social life and is conditioned by social forms, then spirituality is deformed, obscured and enslaved. The ascetic forms of the past were to a great extent determined by the social order. Asceticism assumes different forms under a natural economic system, under a system of slavery or serfdom, under a Capitalist and industrial system. It would probably assume yet another form under Socialism. It is, for example, inadmissible to preach the necessity of fasting to a hungry man. Spirit should make its influence felt on the social environment, while at the same time remaining inwardly independent of it. According to our definition spirit is free from determinism; and determinism, as a rule, implies a want of spirituality, a want of spiritual awareness, a want of purity and freedom. Materialism has confounded spiritual slavery with spiritual essence, the diseased state with the normal one. But it is because spirituality has been divorced from life and relegated to an abstract sphere that both human and religious life have become materialized. Materialism has, in fact, a spiritual origin.

The material domination of human life is the result of a divorce between spirituality and the complete life. It has fostered a bourgeois spirit in the affairs of men. Socialism may fail to save man from bourgeois slavery—it may even help to reinforce it—unless it can rediscover spirit. The reign of the bourgeois involves de-spiritualization, it is a surrender of man to the power of money. Money is the only criterion in a despiritualized world, in a world which has lost all notion of freedom, purpose, creativeness and love. There are two symbols, bread and money; and there are two mysteries, the eucharistic mystery of bread and the satanic mystery of money. We are faced with a great task: to overthrow the rule of money and to establish in its place the rule of bread. Money divorces spirit and world, spirit and bread, spirit and labour. In the first place, money undermines the whole spirit-uality comprehending the whole of human life. Thus severed from the whole life, spirituality is made to justify the power of money and to betray the symbol, bread. In the symbol of bread spirit becomes one with the flesh of the world. The despiritual-ized world worships the symbol of money. The kingdom of money is an objectified kingdom. But the symbol of bread leads to authentic existence. The kingdom of money is fictitious, the kingdom of bread is a return to realities. Socialism is engaged in a struggle against the kingdom of money. But if Socialism itself turns away from spirit and spirituality then it will inevitably prepare the way for another tyranny of money. The reign of money is the realm of worldly power, of bourgeois power. The Socialist State will not differ to any great extent from the bour-geois State unless it is animated by spirit. Spirit, manifest in free-dom, love and purpose, can alone resist the bourgeois kingdom of money, the kingdom of worldly power.

Christianity in the past has failed to produce either a whole spirituality or a whole humanity. The fact that the problem of human labour has not yet been spiritually solved has prevented the emergence of a whole spirituality. Spirituality was relegated to a special sphere where it had no concern with the problem of labour or that of man's physical necessities; the operative solution paid no heed to spirituality and was, in fact, opposed to it. This was not, of course, the way to achieve a whole humanity. The bourgeois Capitalist world was created in a spiritual void, and in it human existence was extremely objectified. But the Socialist world persists in spiritual abstraction, and very often in hostility to spirit. What Marx termed the abstraction of human nature in Capitalist society, I call objectification. But Socialist society can have no way of ending this abstraction and this objectification if it sets out to organize the world regardless of spiritual considerations. The new spirituality must overcome the irreconcilable dualism dividing and disrupting human nature. The old spirituality preferred to confine its awareness of the struggle with evil and with the elemental forces of nature to the realm of asceticism. The modern consciousness, which has strayed away from spirituality, wages this struggle against the forces of evil and nature exclusively with the help of technical weapons and of a technical organization. Thus both the ascetic and the technical solutions of the problem make the integration of human nature impossible; they abstract and thwart spirituality and transform the technically organized world into a soulless wilderness. To deny spirituality is to deny man both his human and Divine image. But at the same time a renouncement of technical achievement, of the social struggle and the advantages of organization, would also be a repudiation and humiliation of man, his enslavement and submission to evil. This is where the new spirituality must strive to be effective, by combining contemplation and activity, spiritual concentration and the will to struggle. It is completely wrong to base the spiritual life on the old antithesis of *spirit* and *flesh*. St. Paul interpreted this as an antithesis between the old and the new man. The new man, the *spiritual* man, does not repudiate the *flesh*, if by that we mean more than simply sin; on the contrary he endeavours to master the *flesh*, in order to illumine and transfigure it into spiritual flesh. This involves a different attitude to social and cosmic life, a different attitude to the problem of labour with which spirituality is inseparably associated. Labour is not only a form of asceticism, it is also a technical and constructive achievement, a sacrifice and a struggle, a penetration of cosmic life; and it is also a form of association, of communication between men. Labour is deeply related to spirituality; it alters the nature of spirituality and makes it more whole. In this consists the relation of spirituality to society. It is high time that a spirituality—a Christian spirituality—were founded in the world. Whatever name we give to it, be it Socialism or Communism, it should be first and foremost a personalistic spirituality, one based upon the relation of one man to another, of one concrete personality to another. This spirituality would defend the human personality against the tyranny of society; it would recognize the sacred right of man to lead an intimate personal life, to live in solitude even if he so desires. When the forms of community and society are admittedly based upon forms of spirituality, then the development of the human character and the improvement of human qualities will become the primary considerations.

IV

As this is a philosophical rather than a theological treatise, I am concerned with spirit as distinguished from the Holy Spirit. It is not my intention to discuss questions of dogma connected with the doctrine of the Holy Spirit. Nevertheless the problem of the Holy Spirit and of His relation to spirit is of fundamental importance to Christian thought. Christianity is *pneuma-centric*. The *pneuma* or spirit is the bearer and source of prophetic inspiration in Christianity. The *paracletism* inherent in Christianity has always encouraged Christians to hope for its revelation, for the advent of a new age of the Holy Spirit. S. Bulgakov very rightly maintains that there can be no personal incarnation of the Holy Spirit, that His incarnation must be universal, diffused throughout the world. Hence the great difficulty of defining the relationship of spirit to the Holy Spirit. The workings of the Holy Spirit are manifest in spirit. Spiritual life is communion with Divine life.

Thus Karl Barth, for instance, regards spirit as the Creator's gift of grace to the creature. He believes that grace is evidence that we were created. The holy Spirit is eschatologically present in man. One of the fundamental contradictions of Barth's teaching is the fact that it limits the potential agency of the Holy Spirit on man and on the world. Roman Catholic theology very nearly identifies the Holy Ghost with grace, though grace has its own principle of action. How do the Holy Scriptures speak of the Holy Spirit? In the first place, it is surprising to note that everything in the Gospel is actuated by and through the agency of the Holy Spirit.

Birth is always an act of spirit. Jesus was born of the spirit, He was baptized by the Holy Spirit, and He was led into the wilderness by the spirit. The agency of the Holy Spirit is spoken of in the Gospel in these words: '*Ye shall not speak, but the Holy Father shall speak in you*' (Matthew x. 20). The Divine Spirit exorcizes devils. '*To sin against the Holy Ghost is the unpardonable sin*' (Matthew xii. 31). '*Ye know not the Spirit*' (Luke ix. 55). '*The Holy Ghost will tell you in that hour what ye shall say*' (Luke xii. 12). '*Ye must be born again of the Spirit to enter into the Kingdom of Heaven*' (John iii. 5). '*The Spirit breathes where it will*' (John iii. 8). '*Spirit revives. The Father will send as a comforter the Holy Spirit*' (John xv. 26). '*He will instruct in all things. The Spirit of truth is apparent in every truth*' (John xvi. 13). '*Everything is made manifest in the spirit. We must school our spirits. The Spirit is truth*' (I Epistle of John). '*All things are judged by the Spirit. The Spirit is in all things. Gifts are by the Spirit. First the Soul, then the Spirit. The letter killeth, but the Spirit maketh to live.*' '*The Lord is the Spirit; where the Spirit is Lord there is liberty*' (II Epistle to Cor. iv. 17). '*Quench not the Spirit*' (I Epistle to Thess. v. 19). The most remarkable statements are: '*The Spirit breathes where it will; where the Spirit is Lord there is liberty; the sin against the Holy Ghost is the unpardonable sin; quench not the spirit.*' The Gospels and the Apostolic Epistles give the impression of being *pan-pneumatic*. The doctrine of the Holy Spirit has hardly been elaborated; there is no trace of it in the Apostolic or the Apologetic literature; it is barely developed by the doctors of the Church, and even then it is usually subordinated. But I have previously said the Holy Spirit is nearest to man, the most immanent, the most universal in action and, at the same time, the least comprehensible and the most mysterious. Perhaps there should be no doctrine of the Holy Spirit, for a doctrine is binding and limiting. Thus the distinction between the Holy Spirit and spirit is a purely doctrinal one. All charisms, all gifts are the spirit's: those of the prophet, the apostle, the saint as well as those of the poet, the philosopher, the inventor, the reformer. The religion of spirit speaks not of justification or salvation, but of the illumination of human nature, of a real change. The invisible kingdom of spirit is created in inscrutable ways, and there are no legal obstacles or limitations in those ways. The agency of spirit is always a victory over human slavery and abasement, a vital surge and ecstasy. Such are the attributes of the Holy Spirit in the Holy Scripture; and such also are the attributes of spirit in the cultural and the social life. St. Simon the New Theologian says that illumination can dispense with written laws. There is a profound antagonism between spirit and law. There is a profound difference between inspiration, charismatism and new birth of early Christianity and the later ascetic schools with their disciplines, laws and stages of perfection. The Holy Spirit and spirit are alike in their agency; they both manifest themselves in inspiration, charismatism and the surge of vital forces. There is a gulf between spirit and authority. The agency of the Holy Spirit and spirit is not continuous and evolutionary, but sporadic and catastrophic.

Authority is of paramount importance in the religious life. It is often invested with religious attributes. But actually questions of authority pertain to the sociological rather than to the pneumatological sphere. Authority is purely a product of objectification and, as such, does not exist in the spiritual life. Authority implies socialization of spirit, a spirituality serving social ends. Authority interprets the spiritual life in the light of social relations, in the light of rulers who govern nations and great ones who exercise authority. But Christ said, 'Let it be not so among you.' Authority is the attribute of the social function of the Church. The need for authority reflects the need for a supreme criterion exalted above the relative and changing plural world, for a superhuman criterion. This is a desire for security and immunity; but these are essentially human aspirations. They are social rather than spiritual aspirations. The spiritual life is perilous and insecure; the path of freedom is beset by risks. Authority implies determination, and is operative only in the externally determined sphere. This is, of course, the social rather than the spiritual sphere. Hegel was not an exemplary Christian, but he was right when he said that spirit was a return to self, that the Holy Spirit was a subjective spirit. Authority is the extreme pole of objectivity, whereas spirit is extreme subjectivity, the very depths of subjectivity. In the sphere of religious or spiritual authority spirit is abstracted from itself and externalized. Thus spiritual authority is a social one; it is the symbol of a humanity which has not yet discovered its essential divinity, which is governed by purely human power relationships. Authority is expressed in human words, conceptions, laws, interests rather than in the ineffable murmurings of spirit and in inspiration. In speech and action authority is represented by popes, assemblies, bishops, social institutions. If any of these were really inspired then authority would be at an end. A spiritual criterion would do away with criteria as such, with the very problem of criteria. There can be no criterion of spirit, since it is itself a criterion. A lower criterion cannot be applied to a higher one; and since authority is by nature social it cannot be a criterion of spirit. Spirit itself leads us in the ways of truth. There is no criterion of what is spirit except spirit itself. It is even an error to seek for a criterion, for that denotes faltering faith and doubt in the agency of spirit. The life of the Church as a social and historical institution is based upon the maxim: Let the powers that be, government, authority, with their guarantees of security, be active whether spirit is active or not. Thus the life of the Church is subject to social determination. It is false to be tempted by sovereign power. All sovereign power is human and is expressed in human words, thoughts and acts. And every human sovereignty is opposed to another human sovereignty. Sovereign power is God's alone. Divine sovereignty is never incarnated, but only the Divine sacrificial love. Ultimately not even God is sovereign, since sovereignty is a human rather than a Divine phenomenon. When God revealed Himself in the world, it was as a poor, not a rich, man; he was incarnated not as the authority, but as the crucified truth of this world. Not being worldly authority God is not a sovereign, for the latter is essentially a human and social phenomenon. God is power rather than authority. Divine power is spiritual and cannot be compared with the manifestations of authority in this world. Spiritual power is freedom. Spiritual power has no need of the authorities of this world; it is a miracle compared with the determinism of this world.

All attempts to discover a criterion of spiritual life, all authoritarian doctrines, are confined to the corrupt sphere of worldly life and have no solution to offer. The most perfect authoritarian doctrine—that of Catholicism—can achieve no real security, for no such thing exists. Catholic doctrine has only succeeded in building up a strongly disciplined authority or, in other words, in demonstrating that authority is associated with the social sphere of religious life. In the last analysis it is impossible to distinguish when the Pope is speaking *ex cathedra* or infallibly, and when he is speaking like any fallible mortal. When the Pope was fallible, and he was often fallible in history, it would appear that he was not acting like an infallible Pope. The implication is that the Pope was infallible only when he uttered infallible truths like any other man. The Pope is infallible when inspired by the Holy Spirit. But there is no criterion to decide when he is so inspired. An even more complicated situation arises when infallible authority is claimed by a council or a synod. A council is infallible only when it is inspired by the Holy Spirit and gives utterance to truth. But there is, again, no criterion for judging when a council is so inspired. Nor is there any criterion of the Holy Spirit. And in any case the Holy Spirit is not a criterion, always a rational and legal concept, but is rather grace, freedom and love. It is independent of any kind of determinism. Khomyakov grasped this fact very well in his doctrine of *Sobornost* which repudiated any external authority. The agency of the Holy Spirit is manifest in *Sobornost*, in the Church as an integral whole, in the Church community. But there are no criteria to establish the fact. We have on the one hand truth, the utterance of a council, and we have on the other the council in which truth is uttered. The Holy Spirit is not revealed in the council, but the council is implied in the revelation of the Holy Spirit. Dostoievsky had an even deeper understanding of the temptation involved in relying upon authority in the spiritual life. In his *Legend of the Grand Inquisitor* he qualified authority as the temptation of the Antichrist. Dostoievsky's discoveries have a bearing not only on Catholicism but also on Orthodoxy, as well as on all religions admitting the principle of authority in the spiritual life. The defenders of authority usually accuse their opponents of repudiating spiritual incarnation and of admitting only the non-incarnated or the reincarnated spirit. This accusation is, however, untrue. Spirit—the Holy Spirit—is incarnated in human life, but it assumes the form of a *whole humanity* rather than of authority. This is, indeed, the pivotal idea of my book. That is the only justification of anthropomorphism as a theosophy, for God is like a whole humanity rather than like nature, society or concept. The agency of the Holy Spirit is not manifest in hierarchy, authority, natural laws, State regulations, or in the determinism of an objective world, but in human existence, creation, inspiration, love and sacrifice. It is an error to identify incarnation and objectification. Social institutions foster the objectification rather than the incarnation of spirit. In the process of objectification the Church has become an idol like the State, like the nation, like everything else that springs out of everyday social life. The Church as a *synagogue* is faced with a terrible crisis, for it is being forsaken by spirit, it has lost its prophetic spirit. And we must hope for a new age of the Holy Spirit. Revelation is always in spirit and is always spiritual, but it is merely symbolized and not realized in the objectified order and in society. Religious revelation is spiritual, and a return to the sources of revelation is a return to spirit and spirituality. Only such a return will not be a reaction. It is an error to say that tradition is authority. Authentic tradition is existential, it is the spiritual life. An established and hidebound tradition is, however, spiritual death.

V

In philosophical terms the new spirituality signifies freedom from objectification and from the subjection of spirit to the influence of a wicked and fallen society. It also implies a transition from spiritual symbolism to spiritual realization. The spiritual life is man's liberation from servitude, from the magic spells of primitive humanity, from the illusions of consciousness and the tyranny of an unconscious hereditary tradition—in fact, from every kind of taboo impeding free agency. The contention of the defenders of the old spirituality that struggle against sin and emancipation from it are the primary considerations does not in the least invalidate the above statement. Sin is, indeed, man's servitude, the loss of spiritual freedom, the submission to external determination. But spirit and spirituality are not in any sense submission to the objectified natural and social orders, or a sanctification of established forms like the Church, the State, property, national life, family, and so forth. Spirit is revolutionary in relation to the world; it is revealed in freedom, justice, love, creativeness, intuitive knowledge rather than in objectified structures—in short, in existential subjectivity rather than in objectivity. A spiritual victory in the world is a victory of subjectivity over objectivity, of the personal and the individual over the general. Objectification of spirit fatally leads to idolatry, for it involves the recognition of social institutions like the Church, the State, the nation, and so on as sacred institutions. Spirit is betrayed and transformed into a conventional symbolism. Real spiritualization is a process of subjectification; it involves an order based on subjectivity, on the existential subject, a personalistic order. Only the existential, anti-historical order based on freedom and love can be a sacred order. The object kills spirit. The object is conventional; it is a symbol rather than a reality. Hence all historic grandeur is vain and ephemeral. In history there is a constant clash of two antithetical principles: subject, spirit, prime reality, freedom, truth, justice, love, humanity are all opposed to object, world, external causality, utility, adaptability, violence and power. This is, indeed, a struggle between God and Caesar. The Son of God and of man was crucified in this world. And in the same way spirit is constantly being crucified in the objectified world; the objectification of spirit is in fact its crucifixion.

Spirit and power are related in a paradoxical way in this world. Spirit is power, and spirit alone is active. Matter is infirm and passive, it is not yet a complete reality. But in the world matter gives the illusion of greater power than spirit. Hartmann has some foundation for his assertion that the most valuable is the weakest of all, and that the least valuable is the strongest of all. The power of the lowest and most material elements lies in the fact that they can do violence, while the most valuable elements, the spiritual and the Divine, cannot do violence. This is part of the objectifying process which assures the predominance of the lowest forces and then sanctifies them. Thus the State is incomparably stronger than the Church, economic forces are stronger than spiritual culture. An army technically well equipped can destroy all before it. In the same way when the Church endeavoured to assert its supremacy in the objectified world, it had to have recourse to means of coercion borrowed from the State. Spirit and spirituality were adapted to an objectified world in which all things tend to assume the forms of material coercion. The objectified world is organized for the benefit of the average man, for everyday social life. The best elements, spirit, creativeness, love, heart, are all crucified in this world. Objectification is the triumph of the average, it is contrary to spiritual ascension. For the benefit of the objectified world a special God has been invented—a God of might and authority comparable in power to the State or to some natural causal force. The development of spirituality implies, however, an emancipation from this particular notion of God, a purification of theology from the lower categories of causality and power. A higher spirituality will prove to be a deathblow to objectivity. The spiritual sphere is the inner subjective sphere, a sphere of freedom and love oblivious of the world of external and abstract causality. But Christian spirituality has assumed the burden of the fallen world as an act of free expiation, as an expression of love and charity. Spirituality disdains obedience, servitude, conformity and compromise with the powers of the world; it looks upon the world in the light of sacrifice and love, of expiation and acceptance of the burden of the world. The new spirituality should appear disincarnate; it should rebel against incarnation as a form of objectification or of historical relativity; but actually it will be a reincarnation, a catastrophic rather than an evolutionary reincarnation.

In the spiritual life there is a struggle between symbolism and realism. The interpretation of symbols as ultimate realities is not only a misunderstanding of symbolism, but also an evil system of servitude. It is a form of naïve realism. In contradistinction true realism is concerned with the knowledge of symbolism, with an awareness of the distinction between symbolism and realism. It is the task of the symbolist theory of knowledge to prepare the way for realism. We must distinguish between *symbolized* and *realized* forms of spirit and spirituality. Symbolism is an important element not only in culture, but also in mysticism. In mysticism we find a symbolism of sexual and generic relationships, terms such as spouse, lover, bride, and so forth. The peculiarity of symbolism consists in its conventional character, in the fact that it becomes a convention at the expense of perpetual creativeness and eventually an instrument of objectification. Realism in the spiritual life implies a perpetual creative process. Spiritual realism is revealed in creativeness, freedom and love. The new spirituality will be realistic; it will be a realism of freedom, activity, creativeness, love, charity, a realism of change and world transfiguration. We cannot dispense with symbolism in language and thought, but we can do without it in the primary consciousness. In describing spiritual and mystical experience men will always have recourse to spatial symbols such as height and depth, to symbols of this or another world. But in real spiritual experience these symbols disappear; there are no symbols of height and depth, of this or another world. The primal creative act is realistic and non-symbolical; it is free from conceptional elaboration. But symbolism begins as soon as the creative act materializes itself in the world. And, in its turn, this symbolism reacts on the spiritual life, giving it a symbolical character. Thus spiritual life is given the imprint of 'cultural' symbolism. Then also spiritual life is defined in relation to *being*, which is already a concept and bears the imprint of conceptional symbolism. When the spiritual life is defined in relation to being, it is defined in relation to the object. The transition from symbolism to realism in the spiritual life is one from objectification to the mystery of existence. This does not imply, of course, an immediate passage to the oneness and identity of Divine life, to the Godhead apophatically interpreted. The spiritual life is a path; on this path a struggle is waged, demanding heroism and sacrifice, an experience of contradiction, schism and disruption. The spiritual life is dialogical, and it has therefore no use for monism. But it does require the confrontation of the human and the Divine, of the human and the Divine wills. The One is not sufficient for the realization of the spiritual life, it has need of another in relation to the One. Realism in the spiritual life will lead inevitably to the purification of the notion of God from all human distortions, from the instincts of power and tyranny, masochism and sadism. It will prove to be a way of spiritualizing theology.

The spiritualization of Christianity is not at an end, it is more than ever necessary. In the world to-day a notion of God, incompatible with a pure conscience and a pure humanity, is being judged. There is a process of liberation from an evil system of symbolism reflecting a clouded state of the human consciousness. In this context atheism itself is, perhaps, but a dialogical moment in the process of theological purification, spiritualization and humanization. Man's notion of God bears the symbolical imprint of his inhumanity. But the purified spiritual life will also be a revelation of Divine humanity. This purer form of spirituality should do away with the physical torments associated with mysticism, it should liberate man from the phantasmagoric and pathological idea that God is moved by human suffering. In the light of this, the whole character of the spiritual life is transformed. God has no need of human suffering, fear and servitude; He only needs men's ascension, their ecstatic transcendence of their limitations. The new spirituality will be first and foremost an experience of creative energy and inspiration. Hence we can discard the symbolism associated with human slavery and humiliation. The aim of the spiritual life is above all to transcend self-limitation and self-centredness, to overcome egocentricity. The personality can only be realized through self-transcendence. But the old spirituality and asceticism left man cloistered within himself, self-absorbed and preoccupied with his own sins and suffering. This gives rise to false symbolisms and illusions of consciousness. Far from being egocentric, spirituality directs man's energies towards his fellow-beings, towards society and the world in general. This is, indeed, the teaching of the Gospel. Spirit liberates man from a false symbolism standing in the way of his realization of life. Spirit liberates man from the burden of self, and no objects can achieve this. Objectivism is another aspect of man's self-centredness, of his inability to transcend himself. Hysterical women are an example of hopeless self-centredness. The inability to perceive realities as distinct from objects, to perceive the Thou and We, to perceive God, is a classic form of egocentricity. Thus hysterical women create an illusory symbolical world of their own, they objectify their own egocentricity and manias. But an element of this is common to every man obsessed by the sin of egocentricity. Thus the dense, compact world of symbolism, which is now the sphere of psycho-pathological research, came into being. Realism is a spiritual victory over egocentricity. The passage from symbolical values to real values is likewise a victory of human dignity and human quality over social hierarchical dignity and quality, a victory of personal dignity over generic dignity, a victory of the human hierarchy over the generic hierarchy, a victory of what man *is* over what man *has*. It is a victory of spiritual freedom over natural and social determinism.

The spiritual life has always been in danger of legalistic deformation, which originates in the process of social objectification and adaptation to everyday life. But the spiritual life is not determined by rules, laws, norms, or general principles. It is, rather, an inner struggle, an experience of freedom, a clash of opposing principles; it is based on a tragic principle postulating contradiction, antagonism, negation. The new spirituality involves purification from extraneous principles, from all forms of compromise with the average and normal consciousness. Hence the new spirituality should reveal the creative essence of spirit and it should justify the purpose of creativeness. It should demonstrate that only spiritual manifestations are free from falsehood, which in worldly affairs is merely a means to an end. Ascetic metaphysics, which replaced the idea of the Kingdom of God by that

M

of personal salvation, also adapted itself to social conditions, for it regarded the world as being both sinful and immutable. But pure Christianity does not repudiate the cosmic world as such, but only the world of untruth, falsehood, hate, slavery and sin. And, moreover, it insists on the necessity of transforming this world, of discovering the Kingdom of God. As I have already said, the Christian Gospel and prophecy are not fundamentally ascetic, but rather Messianic and revolutionary. Perfection is attained not through concentration on self and the salvation of self, but through forgetfulness of self, through renunciation of self, through interest in other men and, finally, through serving the Kingdom of God on earth. In the worldly life the ends and the means are divorced; evil means are made use of to attain good ends. In the spiritual life there can be no distinction between the means and the ends because there is a different attitude to time: the present is no longer a means and the future an end; instead, there are only the instant and eternity. Nor can there be any distinction between theory and practice, for contemplation and eternity are one in the spiritual life. It is the achievement of inner wholeness, of a whole mind or of wisdom. The influence of spirit is ever present in the soul in the form of freedom and grace rather than of causality. For the understanding of the spiritual life it is very important to grasp that the Divine agency, that of the Holy Spirit, that of grace, is not a causal agency. In this consists the mystery of the spiritual life, which is so different from the life of the world. But there were constant attempts to adapt the spiritual life to the conditions of the world, of nature and of society and, in this way, the infirmities of spirit were revealed. This was done because men were afraid, because they longed for immunity and security, which they could find only in the lower sphere of causality, law and authority. Thus security was bought at the expense of the higher life. The spiritual or higher life is beset with dangers. Human selfishness and egocentricity act in such a way as to pervert everything, and they make such harmless qualities as humility and obedience appear dangerous.

Spirit is often opposed to elemental nature, and is made to wage war against it. But as a matter of fact, spirit is less opposed to elemental, primordial and irrational nature than it is to the secondary sphere of objectification and law. The word *nature* can be interpreted in two ways: there is a preconscious existential nature and there is a post-conscious and objectified nature. The first admits of spiritual communion, the latter only of scientific or technical relations. The Romantics had wished to rediscover pre-conscious nature. According to them, man's consciousness of sin, with its consequences of struggle for existence, necessity and slavery, was preceded by a Divine and paradisial state of nature. Anti-spiritualists like Klages fail to grasp this distinction. The new spirituality should interpret nature in the existential way. The old spirituality was too much a part of antiquated forms of philosophy and science as well as old and unacceptable social forms. But spirit cannot be definitely welded to any particular transitory forms of knowledge or society. The liberation of spirit from such transitory forms should be the work of the creative spirit itself. The new spirituality will be the expression of spiritual maturity, of an end of a period of childhood when spirit was still submerged in psychic and natural elements, and bound by law.

We can establish three stages of spirituality: that of natural limitations, that of social limitations and that of a pure, liberated spirituality. Pure, liberated spirituality is at the same time a sign that spirit is becoming master of nature and society. In the past spirituality was thwarted by natural or social influences, by man's dependence on natural or social environment. As a result, spirituality tended to be cosmocratic or sociocratic. In the pagan world spirituality was particularly limited by nature; in the Christian world it was particularly limited by society. Pure spirituality does not sanctify any of life's historical aspects; it holds sacred only God and man's Divine nature, truth, love, charity, justice, beauty, creative inspiration. The natural and social limitations of spirituality involve the problem of the finite and the infinite. These limitations tend to make spirituality finite and hermetic. Finite and objectified are synonymous in the spiritual life. Rationalistic and legalistic modes are the reflection of this tendency in the religious life. The finite principle in the religious life is completely opposed to the prophetic spirit. But we must be careful to distinguish between spiritual and cosmic infinity, for the latter dissolves the personality. We must also distinguish between spiritual infinity and abstract or mathematical infinity. Spiritual infinity is concrete, and is revealed only through a pure and liberated spirituality. An infinite freedom is thus revealed in the spiritual life. This concrete spiritual infinity postulates the end of evil infinity. The spirituality concerned with the end of this world is a prophetic one. But it would be wrong to conceive it as human passivity or as passive expectation. On the contrary it is a most active and highly revolutionary spirituality. The new spirituality is not only concerned with the past, with Christ and the wicked world that crucified Him, but also with the future, with the Second Coming of Christ, with the Kingdom of God. But the Second Coming of Christ, the Kingdom of God are also being prepared by human activity and human creativeness. The end of the world is man's responsibility as well as God's. And the Christ Who was crucified was not only God but also man, an expression of human activity. It is essential to strip the image of Christ from its conventional attributes. The agency of God is also revealed in the world through man, through the human spirit; and in the man Jesus spoke both the Divine and the divinely human voices.

The experience of prophetic spirituality, which is always active and creative, is a fiery appeal to serve the world and humanity, but only on condition of freedom from the world and from social dictates. It is a spirituality which has struggled free from natural and social determinism. The belief in man's Divine nature is common to all religions, although they have often given imperfect expression to this. This was also the *credo* of Philosophers who aspired to spiritual knowledge. In essence this was also the belief of the atheist Feuerbach. Spirit is the Divine element in man, the spiritual element inherent in him. The spiritual life is the new life for which man is thirsting; the *pneuma* is its principle. All man's loftiest aspirations are spiritual. Therefore we must think of the new life in spiritual rather than in natural or social terms. But spirit inwardly accepts both the natural and the social life, endows them with purpose, wholeness, freedom and eternity, and banishes the death and corruption awaiting all non-spiritual things. The belief in immortality is an immediate awareness of our spirituality. The human body itself, as a part of the human personality, is permeated by spirituality and won for eternity. On the threshold of the most profound and ultimate depths we are faced with the revelation that our experience is contained within the depths of the Divine life itself. But at this point silence reigns, for no human language or concept can express this experience. That is the *apophatic* sphere of irreconcilable contradictions baffling human thought. That is the ultimate realm of free and purified spirituality, which no monistic system is capable of defining. On *this side* there remain dualism, tragedy, conflict, man's dialogue with God, the plural world confronted with the One. It is not by discarding the principle of personality that the absolutely Divine One can be attained, but rather by exploring the spiritual depths of the personality which is antinomically united to the One. The purified, liberated spirituality does not imply a renunciation of the personality as part of the plural existence, but of the natural and social limitations connected with objectification. The purified, liberated spirituality is a subjectification—a passage into the sphere of pure existence. The objectified world can be destroyed by man's creative effort, but only because it will also be a manifestation of the Divine agency. In the first place this postulates a change in consciousness, for the phantom world is the creation of a falsely orientated consciousness. But this will not be a form of idealism unconscious of the stress of massive reality, of massive number, of the human mass as well as of the mass of the material world; it will be a form of ascending and descending spiritual realism, active rather than passive in spirit.

INDEX

Actualism, 156, 157
Agnosticism, 124
Alexandrian philosophy, 22
Anaxagoras, 19
Apollonian Principle, 101, 137
Aristotle, 19, 21, 22
Atheism, 97, 123, 153, 172
Atman, 134
Aurelius, Marcus, 99

Bachofen, 36, 41
Barth, Karl, 26, 129, 144, 163
Barthianism, 133
Bergson, 31
Bloy, Léon, 111
Boehme, Jacob, 105, 117, 127
Brahman, 134
Brunschvicg, 31
Buddha, 69
Buddhism, 71, 87, 99, 139
Bulgakov, S., 162

Cabala, 130
Caesar, 169
Calvinism, 133
Capitalism, 37, 94, 161
Carlyle, 111
Cartesianism, 19, 39
Chernishevsky, 70
Clement of Alexandria, 81
Cohen, 31
Communism, 111; Russian, 132, 162
Communist Revolution, 109
Confucius, 69
Constantine the Great, 77

Daltonism, 7
De Man, 158
Dempf, Aloysius, 123

Denifle, 121
Descartes, 72
Dilthey, 31, 45
Dionysian cult, 101, 137
Dionysus, 137
Dostoievsky, 84, 104, 111, 167

Eckhart, Master, 125, 155
Empiricism, 15
Epictetus, 99
Epicurus, 70, 93
Epicureanism, 69
Erasmus, 151
Eudaemonism, 114
Existential philosophy, 9, 32, 153

Fénélon, 138
Feofan the Hermit, Bishop, 83, 88
Feuerbach, 40, 50, 93, 153, 177
Fichte, 9, 18, 27, 30, 131
Franciscanism, 58
Franck, C., 14, 145
French Revolution, 109

Gentile, 30
Gnosticism, 72, 102, 140, 144
Greek Fathers, 140
Greek philosophy, 9, 21, 26, 33
Greek tragedy, 97, 115
Guyon, Madame, 138

Hartmann, N., 30, 44, 45, 169
Hegel, 8, 17, 27, 40, 58, 103, 131, 165
Hegelianism, 27, 40, 44
Heiler, 144
Hellenists, 98
Heraclitus, 130
Herder, 27

179

Hindu philosophy, 23, 71, 75, 99, 124, 134
Hugh of St. Victor, 64
Humanism, 113

Iamblichus, 23
Idealism, 12
Idealism, German, 9, 12, 28, 40, 133
Isaeus, Holy, of Jerusalem, 78

Jansenism, 92, 114
Jaspers, 31
Jesuits, 82
Jesus of Nazareth, 97, 98, 176
Jesus, Society of, 82
Jews, 98
Job, 96
Judaism, 75

Kant, 9, 16, 27, 40, 106, 131
Kantianism, 52
Khomyakov, 167
Kierkegaard, 111, 113, 157
Klages, 40, 137, 175
Krause, 123

Lawrence, D. H., 137
Leibnitz, 98
Leonardo da Vinci, 58
Lossky, 14
Lotze, 31
Luther, 58, 83, 86, 133, 138, 144

Malebranche, 144
Manicheism 72, 103
Marcion, 103
Marx, Karl, 42, 50, 58, 93, 158, 161
Marxism, 58, 115
Materialism, 159
Messianism, 76
Mirandola, Pico della, 33, 151
Molina, L., 82, 138

Molinists, 83
Monophysitism, 132
Mysticism, German, 26, 131, 140

Nechayev, 71
Neo-Kantianism, 8
Neo-Platonism, 22, 71, 75, 99, 125, 140
Neo-Pythagorism, 75
New Testament, 23
Nicolas, of Cusa, 124, 157
Nietzsche, 41, 111, 115, 137
Nigel of Sinai, Holy, 78
Nirvana, 139
Nominalism, 14

Occultism, 143
Oedipus, 97
Orgiasm, 101, 136
Orphism, 71, 75, 99
Otto, R., 134

Pantheism, 127, 132, 134
Paracelsus, 151
Peterson, 145
Philon, 19
Pietism, 145
Plato, 14, 21, 97, 102
Platonism, 15, 19, 105, 135
Plotinus, 10, 40, 71, 117, 125, 134
Plutarch, 22
Pope, The, 83, 166
Positivism, 124
Proclus, 23
Promethean principle, 35
Protestantism, 142
Pseudo-Dionysius, the Areopagite, 84, 125
Psychoanalysis, 143
Puritanism, 114

Quietism, 138

Rachmetov, 70
Realism, 12
Richard of St. Victor, 64
Romantics, 27, 65, 175
Rousseau, Jean Jacques, 90, 138
Rozanov, 62, 137

St. Augustine, 25, 140
St. Bernard, 141
St. Catherine of Siena, 83
St. Francis of Assisi, 58, 141
St. Gregory of Nyssa, 25
St. Gregory of Sinai, 78
St. Ignatius Loyola, 71, 82
St. Irenius, 26
St. Isaac the Syrian, 71, 78
St. John, 25, 79
St. John Cassianus, 78
St. John of the Cross, 123, 141
St. John of the Ladder, 140
St. Ludvina, 83
St. Maxim the Confessor, 79, 125,
  140, 141
St. Paul, 24, 161
St. Seraphim of Sarov, 88, 142
St. Simon the New Theologian, 80,
  122, 142, 164
St. Thomas Aquinas, 27, 37, 125
St. Thomas More, 151
Sakya-Muni, 99
Scheler, 33
Schelling, 8, 27, 131, 133
Schleiermacher, 28
Scholasticism, 12, 21, 25

Schopenhauer, 9, 72, 100, 131
Serapion, Father, 84
Shestov, Léon, 42
Silesius, Angelus, 126
Socialism, 109, 154
Socialist Revolution, 109
Socrates, 97
Solovyev, Vladimir, 86, 97
Sombart, 158
Sophiology, 14
Spencer, 124
Spener, 145
Stoicism, 21, 99, 139
Stoics, 21, 69, 79

Tareyev, 24
Tauler, 126
Tertullian, 26
Theo-Pantheism, 123
Theosophy, 120, 167
Thomism, 12, 21, 83, 105, 121
Titans, 102
Tolstoy, 100, 111, 138
Troeltsch, 158

Universals, The, 14

Voluntarism, 130

Weber, Max, 158
Windelband, 31
Wolff, 27 .

Zossima, Elder, 84

A BRIEF OVERVIEW OF
NIKOLAI BERDYAEV'S LIFE AND WORKS

Nikolai Berdyaev (1874–1948) was one of the greatest religious thinkers of the 20th century. His adult life, led in Russia and in western European exile, spanned such cataclysmic events as the Great War, the rise of Bolshevism and the Russian Revolution, the upsurge of Nazism, and the Second World War. He produced profound commentaries on many of these events, and had many acute things to say about the role of Russia in the evolution of world history. There was sometimes almost no separation between him and these events: for example, he wrote the book on Dostoevsky while revolutionary gunfire was rattling outside his window.

Berdyaev's thought is primarily a religious metaphysics, influenced not only by philosophers like Kant, Hegel, Schopenhauer, Solovyov, and Nietzsche, but also by religious thinkers and mystics such as Meister Eckhart, Angelus Silesius, Franz van Baader, Jakob Boehme, and Dostoevsky. The most fundamental concept of this metaphysics is that of the *Ungrund* (a term taken from Boehme), which is the pure potentiality of being, the negative ground essential for the realization of the novel, creative aspects of existence. A crucial element of Berdyaev's thought is his philosophical anthropology: A human being is originally an "ego" out which a "person" must develop. Only when an ego freely acts to realize its own concrete essence, rather than abstract or arbitrary goals, does it become a person. A society that furthers the goal of the development of egos into persons is a true community, and the relation then existing among its members is a sobornost.

He showed an interest in philosophy early on, at the age of fourteen reading the works of Kant, Hegel, and Schopenhauer.

183

While a student at St. Vladimir's University in Kiev, he began to participate in the revolutionary Social-Democratic movement and to study Marxism. In 1898, he was sentenced to one month in a Kiev prison for his participation in an anti-government student demonstration, and was later exiled for two years (1901–02) to Vologda, in the north of Russia.

His first book, *Subjectivism and Individualism in Social Philosophy* (1901), represented the climax of his infatuation with Marxism as a methodology of social analysis, which he attempted to combine with a neo-Kantian ethics. However, as early as 1903, he took the path from "Marxism to idealism," which had already been followed by such former Marxists as Peter Struve, Sergey Bulgakov, and S.L. Frank. In 1904 Berdyaev became a contributor to the philosophical magazine *New Path*. The same year he married Lydia Trushcheva, a daughter of a Petersburg lawyer. In 1905–06, together with Sergey Bulgakov, he edited the magazine *Questions of Life*, attempting to make it the central organ of new tendencies in the domains of socio-political philosophy, religious philosophy, and art. The influence exerted upon him by the writers and philosophers Dmitry Merezhkovsy and Zinaida Gippius, during meetings with them in Paris in the winter of 1907–08, led him to embrace the Russian Orthodox faith. After his return to Russia, he joined the circle of Moscow Orthodox philosophers united around the Path publishing house (notably Bulgakov and Pavel Florensky) and took an active part in organizing the religious-philosophical Association in Memory of V. Solovyov. An important event in his life at this time was the publication of his article "Philosophical Truth and the Truth of the Intelligentsia" in the famous and controversial collection *Landmarks* (1909), which subjected to a critical examination the foundations of the world-outlook of the left-wing Russian intelligentsia. Around this time, Berdyaev published a work which inaugurated his life-long exploration of the concept of freedom in its many varieties and ramifications. In *The Philosophy of Freedom* (1911), a critique of the "pan-gnoseologism" of recent German and Russian philosophy led Berdyaev to a search for an authentically Christian ontology. The end result of this search was a philosophy of freedom, according to which human beings are rooted in a sobornost of being and thus possess true knowledge.

In 1916, Berdyaev published the most important work of his early period: *The Meaning of the Creative Act*. The originality of this work is rooted in the rejection of theodicy as a traditional problem of the Christian consciousness, as well as in a refusal to accept the view that creation and revelation have come to an end and are complete. The central element of the "meaning of the creative act" is the idea that man reveals his true essence in the course of a continuing creation realized jointly with God (a theurgy). Berdyaev's notion of "theurgy" (in contrast to those of Solovyov and Nikolai Fyodorov) is distinguished by the inclusion of the element of freedom: the creative act is a means for the positive self-definition of freedom not as the choice and self-definition of persons in the world but as a "foundationless foundation of being" over which God the creator has no power.

Berdyaev's work from 1914 to 1924 can be viewed as being largely influenced by his inner experience of the Great War and the Russian Revolution. His main themes during this period are the "cosmic collapse of humanity" and the effort to preserve the hierarchical order of being (what he called "hierarchical personalism"). Revolutionary violence and nihilism were seen to be directly opposed to the creatively spiritual transformation of "this world" into a divine "cosmos." In opposing the chaotic nihilism of the first year of the Revolution, Berdyaev looked for support in the holy ontology of the world, i.e., in the divine cosmic order. The principle of hierarchical inequality, which is rooted in this ontology, allowed him to nullify the main argument of the leveling ideology and praxis of Communism—the demand for "social justice." Berdyaev expressed this view in his *Philosophy of Inequality* (1923).

During this period, Berdyaev posed the theme of Russian

messianism in all its acuteness. Torn apart by the extremes of apocalyptic yearning and nihilism, Russia is placed into the world as the "node of universal history" (the "East-West"), in which are focused all the world's problems and the possibility of their resolution, in the eschatological sense. In the fall of the monarchy in February 1917, Berdyaev saw an opportunity to throw off the provincial Russian empire which had nothing in common with Russia's messianic mission. But the Russian people betrayed the "Russian idea" by embracing the falsehood of Bolshevism in the October Revolution. The Russian messianic idea nevertheless remains true in its ontological core despite this betrayal.

In the fall of 1919, Berdyaev organized in Moscow the Free Academy of Spiritual Culture, where he led a seminar on Dostoevsky and conducted courses on the Philosophy of Religion and the Philosophy of History. This latter course became the basis of one of his most important works: *The Meaning of History: An Essay on the Philosophy of Human Destiny* (1923). His attacks against the Bolshevik regime became increasingly intense: he called the Bolsheviks nihilists and annihilators of all spiritual values and culture in Russia. His activities and statements, which made him a notable figure in post-revolutionary Moscow, began to attract the attention of the Soviet authorities. In 1920, he was arrested in connection with the so-called "tactical center" affair, but was freed without any consequences. In 1922, he was arrested again, but this time he was expelled from Russia on the so-called "philosopher's ship" with other ideological opponents of the regime such as Bulgakov, Frank, and Struve.

Having ended up in Berlin, Berdyaev gradually entered the sphere of post-War European philosophy; he met Spengler, von Keyserling, and Scheler. His book *The New Middle Ages: Reflections on the Destiny of Russia and Europe* (1924) (English title: *The End of Our Time*) brought him European celebrity. Asserting that modern history has come to an end, and that it has been a failure, Berdyaev again claimed that Russia (now the post-revolutionary one) had a messianic mission. He wrote that "culture is now not just European; it is becoming universal. Russia, which had stood at the center of East and West, is now—even if by a terrible and catastrophic path—acquiring an increasingly palpable world significance, coming to occupy the center of the world's attention" (*The New Middle Ages*, p. 36). In 1924, Berdyaev moved to Paris, where he became a founder and professor of the Russian Religious-Philosophical Academy. In 1925, he helped to found and became the editor of the Russian religious-philosophical journal *Put'* (*The Path*), arguably the most important Russian religious journal ever published. He organized interconfessional meetings of representatives of Catholic, Protestant, and Orthodox religious-philosophical thought, with the participation of such figures as Maritain, Mounier, Marcel, and Barth.

In the émigré period, his thought was primarily directed toward what can be called a liberation from ontologism. Emigration became for him an existential experience of "rootless" extra-hierarchical existence, which can find a foundation solely in "the kingdom of the Spirit," i.e., in the person or personality. The primacy of "freedom" over "being" became the determining principle of his philosophy, a principle which found profound expression in his book *On the Destiny of Man: An Essay on Paradoxical Ethics* (1931), which he considered his "most perfect" book. This is how he expressed this principle: "creativeness is possible only if one admits freedom that is not determined by being, that is not derivable from being. Freedom is rooted not in being but in 'nothingness'; freedom is foundationless, is not determined by anything, is found outside of causal relations, to which being is subject and without which being cannot be understood" (from his autobiography, the Russian version, *Self-knowledge*, p. 231).

At around the same time, Berdyaev re-evaluated Kant's philosophy, arriving at the conclusion that only this philosophy "contains the foundations of a true metaphysics." In particular, Kant's "recognition that there is a deeper reality hidden behind the world of phenomena" helped Berdyaev formulate a key principle of his personalism: the doctrine of "objectification," which he first systematically developed in *The World of Objects: An Essay on the Philosophy of Solitude and Social Intercourse* (1934) (English title: *Solitude and Society*). This is how Berdyaev explained this doctrine: "Objectification is an epistemological interpretation of the fallenness of the world, of the state of enslavement, necessity, and disunitedness in which the world finds itself. The objectified world is subject to rational knowledge in concepts, but the objectification itself has an irrational source" (*Self-knowledge*, p. 292). Using man's creative powers, it is possible to pierce this layer of objectification, and to see the deeper reality. Man's "ego" (which knows only the objectified world) then regains its status of "person," which lives in the non-objectified, or real, world. Berdyaev had a strong sense of the unreality of the world around him, of his belonging to another—real—world.

After the Second World War, Berdyaev's reflections turned again to the role of Russia in the world. His first post-war book was *The Russian Idea: The Fundamental Problems of Russian Thought of the 19th Century and the Beginning of the 20th Century* (1946), in which he tried to discover the profound meaning of Russian thought and culture. Himself being one of the greatest representatives of this thought and culture, he saw that the meaning of his own activity was to reveal to the western world the distinctive elements of Russian philosophy, such as its existential nature, its eschatalogism, its religious anarchism, and its obsession with the idea of "Divine humanity."

Berdyaev is one of the greatest religious existentialists. His philosophy goes beyond mere thinking, mere rational conceptualization, and tries to attain authentic life itself: the profound layers of existence that touch upon God's world. He directed all of his efforts, philosophical as well as in his personal and public life, at replacing the kingdom of this world with the kingdom of God. According to him, we can all attempt to do this by tapping the divine creative powers which constitute our true nature. Our mission is to be collaborators with God in His continuing creation of the world.

Summing up his thought in one sentence, this is what Berdyaev said about himself: "Man, personality, freedom, creativeness, the eschatological-messianic resolution of the dualism of two worlds—these are my basic themes."

BORIS JAKIM

2009

BIBLIOGRAPHY OF NIKOLAI BERDYAEV'S
BOOKS IN ENGLISH TRANSLATION
(IN ALPHABETICAL ORDER)

The Beginning and the End. Russian edition 1947. First English edition 1952.

The Bourgeois Mind and Other Essays. English edition 1934.

Christian Existentialism. A Berdyaev Anthology. 1965.

Christianity and Anti-Semitism. Russian edition 1938. First English edition 1952.

Christianity and Class War. Russian edition 1931. First English edition 1933.

The Destiny of Man. Russian edition 1931. First English edition 1937.

The Divine and the Human. Russian edition 1952. First English edition 1947.

Dostoevsky: An Interpretation. Russian edition 1923. First English edition 1934.

Dream and Reality: An Essay in Autobiography. Russian edition 1949. First English edition 1950.

The End of Our Time. Russian edition 1924. First English edition 1933.

The Fate of Man in the Modern World. First Russian edition 1934. English edition 1935.

Freedom and the Spirit. Russian edition 1927. First English edition 1935.

Leontiev. Russian edition 1926. First English edition 1940.

The Meaning of History. Russian edition 1923. First English edition 1936.

The Meaning of the Creative Act. Russian edition 1916. First English edition 1955.

The Origin of Russian Communism. Russian edition 1937. First English edition 1937.

The Realm of Spirit and the Realm of Caesar. Russian edition 1949. First English edition 1952.

The Russian Idea. Russian edition 1946. First English edition 1947.

Slavery and Freedom. Russian edition 1939. First English edition 1939.

Solitude and Society. Russian edition 1934. First English edition 1938.

Spirit and Reality. Russian edition 1946. First English edition 1937.

Towards a New Epoch. Transl. from the original French edition 1949.

Truth and Revelation. English edition 1954.

CPSIA information can be obtained
at www.ICGtesting.com
Printed in the USA
BVHW030857281221
624861BV00012B/57